Milk Glass

Imperial Glass Corporation

Plus Opaque, Slag & More

Myrna & Bob Garrison

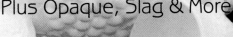

Schiffer Publishing Ltd

4880 Lower Valley Road, Atglen, PA 19310 USA

Dedication

To our children,
Robert and Jenny
Janna and Kirkby
and our grandchildren,
Kendra, Nathan, Matthew, and Scott

To all of our "glass collecting friends." You are friends that we treasure.

Parts of this book appeared in a slightly different version as *Imperial's Vintage Milk Glass* ©
1992 by Myrna and Bob Garrison.
The authors wish to extend appreciation to Lancaster Colony Corporation for permission to
publish photographs and documents of the former Imperial Glass Corporation.
The authors wish to extend appreciation to The Pillsbury Company for permission to use
images from the *Pillsbury Bake Off Dessert Cookbook*, © 1968 with second printing 1971.

Designed by Bonnie M. Hensley
Cover designed by Bruce M. Waters
Type set in ZapfHumanist Dm BT/Korinna BT

ISBN: 0-7643-1262-6
Printed in China
1 2 3 4

Published by Schiffer Publishing Ltd.
4880 Lower Valley Road
Atglen, PA 19310
Phone: (610) 593-1777; Fax: (610) 593-2002
E-mail: Schifferbk@aol.com
Please visit our web site catalog at **www.schifferbooks.com**

In Europe, Schiffer books are distributed by Bushwood Books
6 Marksbury Avenue Kew Gardens
Surrey TW9 4JF England
Phone: 44 (0) 20-8392-8585; Fax: 44 (0) 20-8392-9876
E-mail: Bushwd@aol.com
Free postage in the UK. Europe: air mail at cost.

This book may be purchased from the publisher.
Include $3.95 for shipping. Please try your bookstore first.
We are always looking for people to write books on new and related subjects.
If you have an idea for a book please contact us at the Atglen, PA. address.
You may write for a free catalog.

Contents

Acknowledgments 4
Preface 5
A Guide to Using This Book 7

Part I: Historical Perspective

A Short History of The Imperial Glass Corporation 9
The Story of Hand-Made Milk Glass 12
Imperial Milk Glass 14

Part II: Decorations and Variations

Belknap Collection 17
Atterbury Molds 18
Hand Decorated—1950 20
Decorated Sugar and Cream Sets—1955 23
Decorated with Violets—1958-1959 25
Hand Decorated Concord Grape—1960s 26
Hand Decorated Coach Lamp Candy Jars—1958-1959 27
Gold Flecked Milk Glass—1954-1957 31
Antiqued Milk Glass—1961-1962 33
Vigna Vetro Milk and Colored Glass Mixed—1959-1960 . 34
Black Glass with Milk Glass Combination—1953-1955 .. 35
Milk Glass and Metal—1953-1961 37
Opaque Glass—1955-1959 43
Black Glass.. 47
Slag Glass 50
Milk Glass with Colored Glass 58
White Ice—1977 64
Milk Glass Heisey Animals—1977-1978, 1988 65
Swung Vases 66
Private Mold Work 67
Undocumented Items 70

Part III: Imperial Patterns and Categories

Patterns—Photographs and Catalog Illustrations 76
    "Candlewick" 76
    Cape Cod 79
    Grape 81
    Hobnail 97
    Lace Edge and "Lace Edge Cut" 102
    "Leaf" and "Leaf Open" 108
    Rose 111
    Scroll 113
    Windmill 115

Categories—Photographs and Catalog Illustrations 116
    Animals and Animal Related 116
    Baskets 121
    Bowls, Plates and Trays 122
    Candy and Cake Stands 125
    Candleholders and Lamps 128
    Cigarette Items 130
    Comportes and Condiments 133
    Decanters and Sets 135
    Salt and Pepper Sets 136
    Cream and Sugar Sets 136
    Vases 139
    Miscellaneous 144

Closing Thoughts 150
Endnotes 152
Appendix I: Where the Molds Are 153
Appendix II: Price Guide by Mold Number 154
Index.. 160

Acknowledgments

To the Imperial Glass Corporation, who made all of this wonderful glass that continues to please people long after the factory ceased.

To Kathy Burch, our long-time Imperial friend, who has spent hours, days, and weeks talking Imperial Glass. Without her friendship, our collecting and researching might have faded.

To Helen and Bill Clark for sharing Imperial records, for contributing needed information to make this book more complete, and for their continued friendship.

To Lucile Kennedy for her generosity of knowledge of Imperial glass and for her encouragement to pursue our research.

And to the late Tommie Carroll who shared her love and knowledge of Imperial Glass through her conversations with us and through the loan of her written material that enabled us to start our research of Imperial Glass.

To the friends who have helped by—sharing glass for photos, pricing, proofreading, talking, listening, and finding pieces for all of our collections. To David and Ruth Adkisson, Rod and Irene Dockery, Mary and Tom Stevenson, Jim and Bev Harris, Max Miller, Keith Burkart, Paul Gould, Frank Chiarenza, Gordon and Juanita McNutt, and Norma Boren for their contributions.

Thanks to Donna Baker, our editor from beginning to finish, for making a difficult task more pleasant. She did a wonderful job of suggesting changes and finding small inconsistencies, always maintaining a positive and cheerful attitude throughout the process of bringing this book to fruition.

Preface

Most collectors are familiar with some patterns of glass for which the Imperial Glass Corporation was famous. However, collectors are not always aware of the amount and the many types of glass that the company produced. In 1978, my husband and I became avid collectors of Imperial Glass, particularly the Cape Cod and Candlewick patterns. We made our first trip to the Imperial factory in 1980 and wrote our first book, *Imperial Cape Cod: Tradition to Treasure,* in 1982. We had already met Mrs. Tommie Carroll, a former Imperial Representative (now deceased), at the Dallas Trade Mart. She was instrumental in our early research by lending us her catalogs and other printed material.

On that first trip to the factory in 1980, we met Miss Lucile Kennedy, Assistant to the President of Imperial Glass Corp. Miss Kennedy opened her office and records to us, and thus supplied us with a wealth of data to draw upon in researching our first book. She continues to encourage us in our research.

In the period since 1980, we have missed only one year making a trip to the factory. In addition, we joined the National Imperial Glass Collectors' Society and became acquainted with other collectors of Imperial glass. We have made strong and lasting friendships within that group, and the annual NIGCS Convention is a reunion we do not want to miss.

Due to financial hardships, the Imperial Company began to sell wares from its archives and basement storage area in 1983. We were fortunate enough to have made several friends among the Imperial employees, and they helped us look into and buy from special reserves. While we were searching in the basement, a friend stepped forward to help us. Helen Clark of the accounting department came down to bring us a flashlight for our hunt. That beam is still burning today as Helen continues to shed light on our many questions!

By 1991, we had found many more items of the Cape Cod pattern, and enough material and information to publish a new, revised edition of *Imperial Cape Cod: Tradition to Treasure.* Even as we researched the first Cape Cod book, however, our interest in milk glass began to intensify. Thus, while the updating of the Cape Cod book took precedence, we also made voluminous notes on milk glass production by Imperial, as we searched their records prior to the 1982 bankruptcy. In 1992, our next book, *Imperial's Vintage Milk Glass,* made its appearance. We believe this book is of interest to both milk glass collectors and Imperial Glass collectors, because a great many of the six hundred plus molds used to produce milk glass items were subsequently reissued in the many of the beautiful colors that Imperial created.

We had been collecting Candlewick and Cape Cod glass perfumes and colognes for a long time. Then we starting adding milk glass colognes and found that we were hunting for other Imperial boudoir items as well. We shared our finds with Helen Clark, and discussed with her the relevant facts of each. As always, Helen came to the rescue with pertinent information that she had. She also spent time helping us find new items, to the point that she called us when she heard of pieces for sale. One day in 1990, Helen called about the sale of several colognes that Imperial made for Irving W. Rice. Naturally, we bought them. Four hundred plus items later, we are completely hooked!

During the years since the closing of Imperial, Helen has shared with us notes and records about the Irving W. Rice Company. In the fall of 1993, we went to the Rakow Library at the Corning Glass Museum to research all the Imperial Glass records. With the help of this material and the invaluable information on the Irving W. Rice card file supplied by Helen, we were able to build a substantial data bank of documented material. The publication of *Imperial's Boudoir, Etcetera . . . A Comprehensive Look at Dresser Accessories for Irice and Others* © 1996 allowed us to share another of Imperial's contributions to the glass world.

Now we have arrived at the need for an updated book on Imperial's milk glass. With our first book on this subject sold out, a few undocumented items to report on, several pieces to photograph which were not pictured previously, and a desire to include the wonderful milk glass boudoir pieces, we decided to undertake a second version of *Imperial's Vintage Milk Glass.*

As in all of our research, we have used Imperial's catalogs to assemble charts of each mold number, with the catalog and price lists in which it appeared for sale. In this manner, we could determine approximately in what year an item was introduced and when it was last cataloged for sale. We feel that these dates of production add a unique facet to a collector's knowledge, and aid in the building of a collection. How long a piece remained in production helps determine a value. Naturally, a piece may have been produced before it was shown in a catalog, just as a piece was usually still available for order after being dropped from the catalog. However, researchers and collectors usually think of production dates as being from the first time an item was cataloged until the last time it was cataloged.

There will always be questions in regard to the research methods used in any project. We have tried to deal with catalog *facts* and not undocumented theories. Our dates were established by using the written material that was available. Due to fewer company catalogs and records prior to 1950, earlier detailed dates are impossible.

Seek, find, enjoy.

A Guide to Using This Book

First and very important is the fact that there is a great amount of helpful information in the text of this book. Collectors need to study this information to understand just how many different treatments Imperial used for their milk glass. Also, one needs to realize that the approximately six hundred items of milk glass were produced in a variety of other colors during Imperial's eighty years of production as well. More designs were incorporated in the milk glass line than in any other line that Imperial produced.

The main purpose of this book is to help you identify items in the company's milk glass line. Slag, opaque and decorated glass are discussed as well because they are often considered to be in the milk glass group. Imperial did not think that milk glass was any color other than white, but the company would most likely be proud to see its slag and opaque items being collected by milk glass lovers today! Occasionally, a hand-decorated milk glass piece might be questionable if it were not documented as being a company product.

Part I of this book provides collectors with a brief historical overview of the Imperial Glass Corporation, of milk glass itself, and of Imperial's milk glass production. Part II is organized chronologically and covers the many decorations and treatments used by the company, as well as pieces made for private mold customers and undocumented items. Part III provides a comprehensive look at the numerous patterns and categories used in the production of Imperial's milk glass. Each pattern and category in Part III is shown through photographs of representative items as well as through complete catalog listings and illustrations.

Mold Numbers, Measurements, Names, and Dates

Keep in mind that when we give a listing of items, we will first list the mold number, then the description, the pattern name, and the years of production. Other pertinent information will be included when useful.

Imperial used the prefix 1950/ for glossy milk glass and 1952/ for their Doeskin treatment (see chapter on "Imperial Milk Glass" for information on Doeskin). To simplify the reading of this book, only the 1950/ prefix is used in the hundreds of listings, although most items were made in both finishes. When known, the exception to this dual production will be noted.

As mentioned later in the book, the prefix 11/ indicates milk glass before 1950 and the prefix 1950/ is the identification number after 1950. As accurately as possible, these items have been cross-referenced.

When known and when appropriate, the Lenox five-digit computer identification number will follow the item description. When there is an early number (prefix 11/) for an item that also had a 1950/ number, both numbers will be shown.

Collectors are sometimes troubled by the meaning of certain descriptive words. For example, Imperial used the word "compote" in some instances and "comporte" at other times. These terms have the same meaning: a bowl, with a base or stem, used to serve fruit, nuts, or sweets. Pokal is a mug, jug, or jar; a large goblet usually covered and typically made of glass.

It is important to bear in mind that Imperial sometimes gave an item one name for a period of time, then changed the name slightly in a later catalog. You will find some of these name changes in our references. We have tried to be consistent, but at the same time we have had to present the actual names and terms used by Imperial. Sometimes, given the number of items in this book plus the number of various treatments used by Imperial, cross referencing all these facts seemed like an impossible task!

Often Imperial used mold numbers only to identify an item. To make identification easier for collectors, we have given pattern names to groups that exhibit similar distinctions. When the names are in quotation marks (for example, "Lace Edge Cut" or "Leaf"), it indicates that the name is not a company name but one that was supplied by us.

Measurements given by Imperial in their description of items sometimes refer to the height and sometimes refer to the width. We always give the measurements and descriptions as Imperial used them.

The dates—when an item was introduced and when it was dropped from production—are guides to how difficult an item will be to find. The shorter the production time, the more difficult it will be to find a certain item. A brief production time will also greatly influence prices. A date of 1930s represents items shown in early, undated catalog pages. The dates 1932 and 1943 are dated price lists.

Pricing

The price guide in this book is just that—a guide. It has been compiled by using prices seen on pieces for sale in antique malls, shops, shows, and similar places in various locations (an asterisk has been used when there was too little information to conclusively determine an item's price). In the past several years the prices for the more common pieces have remained stable while the prices for the covered animal dishes have increased considerably. As so aptly stated by a friend, "Prices are in the eyes of the beholder." We say, "Judge a price by demand, desirability, and the length of time an item was produced."

Part I

Historical Perspective

A Short History of The Imperial Glass Company

"Pride of workmanship, skill, and a deep devotion to quality were the prime motivators of Imperial's glass-workers."

A group of investors organized the Imperial Glass Company in 1901. After a period of "several years of construction, installing furnaces, and creating a number of initial moulds," the first Imperial glass was produced in 1904 in Bellaire, Ohio.

Imperial's earliest production was clear pressed glass. Sales were made to the five and dime stores for items such as covered butter dishes, berry bowls, and pickle dishes. These lines expanded into lamp shades, jelly glasses, pitchers, salt and pepper shakers, sugars and creamers, and other similar types of glass.

The period from 1910 to 1929 saw several new Imperial lines. First was Nuart iridescent ware. In this group were the colored and frosted electric lamp shades in an imitation "Tiffany" style. Following Nuart, Imperial introduced Nucut Crystal, which was a handpressed reproduction of English cut glass. (Collectors Crystal was a reintroduction (1950s) of the Nucut and was one of Imperial's most popular giftware lines.)

"Imperial Jewels . . . exquisite freehand iridescent 'stretch glass' items" were introduced in 1916. This was a "high point" of Imperial's production that involved many shops making pressed wares as well as blown and free-hand ware.

From 1904 to 1922, the company flourished, though the market changed as machine made glassware came to the forefront. In 1922, the mass-produced glass markets caused Imperial to try new ideas, including the creation of Imperial's "Art Glass," an innovation that proved to be unsuccessful.

In 1929, the forces of the Depression, combined with further loss of major markets, forced Imperial to enter bankruptcy. The company continued operations while in receivership, and with an order from Quaker Oats Company in 1931 for a premium to be packaged in its product, Imperial was able to stay in business. The company was reorganized and named the Imperial Glass Corporation.

The Quaker Oats premium was the forerunner of today's Cape Cod pattern, a line that survived until the demise of Imperial in 1984. Another jewel to continue until the closing in 1984 was Candlewick, a pattern that was introduced in 1936. Candlewick contained the largest number of items in any Imperial line. It eventually became more popular than the earlier favorite, Cape Cod.

A 1930s catalog pictured thirty pieces of opal glass from this time period. According to the only 1930s price list available, Imperial produced twenty-four pieces of opal glass in 1932. These are the earliest company documentations found of milk glass produced by the Imperial Glass Company. The height of milk glass production of approximately six hundred items was in the 1950s, with production falling off to less than forty items made after 1970. February 1, 1951, was the introduction of the famous superimposed IG hallmark that was in use for twenty-three years. This mark is often found on Imperial milk glass items.

Imperial had many private mold customers. Companies and individuals brought their molds to Imperial for glass items to be specially made. Imperial also supplied items from its own lines to many different distributors and private mold customers, who then added decorations and marketed these items under their companies' names. A few of these companies were Sears Roebuck Inc., F.W. Woolworth, Butler Brothers, Lightolier [Lighting] Company, Keystone Silver, Inc. Midwest Chandelier Company and Irving W. Rice, Inc.

At the beginning of World War II, changes began taking shape in imports. American companies could no longer import glass products from European countries. Irving W. Rice, New York, was a major importer of colognes and powder boxes. With the onset of the war, Irving W. Rice turned to Imperial Glass Corporation to supply the dresser items for which I. Rice was so well known. The year 1939 was the beginning of a long and strong relationship between the two companies that continued through the 1940s. Correspondence in the late 1960s suggested that the two companies were attempting to resume relations. In 1972, however, when

Lenox bought Imperial Glass Corporation, all private mold work was ceased.

Imperial began acquiring glass companies in 1940. The first purchase was Central Glass Works (1940), followed by the purchase of the molds from the A.H. Heisey Company (1958). Two lines from the Heisey Company became strong Imperial lines: Heisey Provincial and Old Williamsburg were produced by Imperial in crystal as well as colors. The purchase of Cambridge Glass Company (1960) added Rosepoint and a strong line of candelabra.

World War II and the postwar period were the boom years of Imperial's production. Not surprisingly, the peak of production of Cape Cod and Candlewick was reached and sustained during this time. Contributing to this success were the countless thousands of households being established by young families after the war, and the prosperous American economy, which followed.

In 1972, seeing the need for capital investment, Imperial stockholders arranged a stock exchange with Lenox Incorporated. This was accomplished on December 29, 1972, and in 1973 Lenox began marking Imperial glass with an "LIG" mark. In June 1981, Arthur Lorch, a private investor, purchased the company from Lenox. The new mark, "ALIG", began appearing in 1982 and was used only during that year. In the fall of 1982, Lenox foreclosed on its note with Mr. Lorch.

Mr. Robert F. Stahl, Jr., a management consultant, bought the company in late 1982 and filed for Chapter 11 bankruptcy in an effort to reorganize the company. A small amount of glass produced carried the NI mark (superimposed) for "New Imperial." The last day of general production was June 15, 1984. Appropriately, the last item off the production line was a 4" swan with 6-15-84 in raised numbers on the inside. In August 1984, after all efforts failed, liquidation was ordered. Consolidated Liquidation Company and Lancaster Colony combined to purchase the assets of Imperial Glass Corporation and proceeded to sell the last remnants of the bankrupt business. Liquidation was completed with the sale of the building to Mrs. Anna Maroon in March 1985.

The following marks are those used by Imperial to mark its wares. These are the dates the marks were actually registered, or are generally accepted as used for the first time. We do not have registration records for Nuart, but it preceded the Nucut mark.

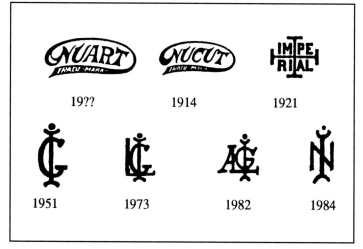

These are the various marks used by the Imperial Glass Corporation from 1904 to 1984. The superimposed IG is the most famous and widely known. It was also used for the longest time period.

Mrs. Maroon invested much time and money trying to find a business to occupy the defunct Imperial factory building. It was her desire to provide an economic stimulus to Bellaire, Ohio, and at the same time preserve this historical building, which meant so much to so many people for many years. The anchor of this endeavor was the Imperial Hay Shed. Originally, the Hay Shed had been the storage place for hay used in packing glass to be shipped. During the later years, the Hay Shed was an outlet for research and development pieces and factory seconds. From 1985 to 1995, the Hay Shed was an Imperial glass consignment shop that was often the first stop for collectors attending the annual convention of the National Imperial Glass Collectors' Society.

The Bellaire Glass and Artifacts Museum played a vital part in drawing visitors to the partially renovated factory building. There were other tenants, but not enough to fulfill the dream of saving the Imperial Glass Corporation factory building, and the building was razed in June 1995. The Hay Shed outlet was moved to a building on adjacent property. On the ground where the Imperial Glass Corporation once stood, now stands a shopping center. A blacktop parking lot now covers the area where collectors once spent hours

This photo was made June 24, 1984, just ten days after the last run of regular production was made at Imperial Glass Corporation.

and days searching for shards and reminiscing about the greatness of Imperial Glass.

We wrote in our first book, *Imperial Cape Cod: Tradition to Treasure*, that " . . . as collectors of Imperial Glass, we have a strong feeling that Imperial will never lose its identity as a producer of fine crystal. In a mass production world, 'Imperial continues to create only handcrafted glassware. Pride of workmanship, skill, and a deep devotion to quality are the prime motivators of Imperial's glassworkers.'" With the close of Imperial, this should be restated: "Imperial continued to create only handcrafted glassware. Pride of workmanship, skill, and a deep devotion to quality were the prime motivators of Imperial's glassworkers."

Quoted parts of this history have been condensed from *A Consumer and Retail Guide to Handcrafted Glassware*, Imperial Glass Corp. Bellaire, Ohio 43906. Remaining information was obtained through printed information from old records of the Imperial Glass Corporation.

The Story of Hand-Made Milk Glass

Knowledge of the beginning of milk glass is necessary before one undertakes a study of Imperial's milk glass. This story was most aptly told by Imperial Glass Corporation in their 1951 pamphlet *The Story of Hand-Made Milk Glass*. To try and summarize or rephrase would be an injustice to this part of the Imperial Glass Corporation's history:

Glass, that indispensable material of modern civilization, was probably first produced over three to five thousand years ago. The earliest history of glass is still incomplete and perhaps will always remain rather sketchy.

In Genesis IV, 22, we find that Tubal-Cain (born 3870 B.C.) son of Zillah and Lamech and the eighth man after Adam, was proficient in the working of brass and iron. The use of fire and clay ovens for melting was already known and slags necessarily formed. Slags are glassy and opaque. Milk glass may have been first formed in some of these materials. The Book of Job XXVIII, 17, philosophizing on "Wisdom" reads 'She cannot be estimated after gold and glass, etc." Solomon's Proverbs mention glass.

. . . Glass was made in Egypt in 1500 B.C. though some specimens are said to date back to 3300 B.C. Early Egyptian products included enamels, mosaics and beads in all of which white glass, resembling the milk glass of today, was included. Onyx, agate and alabaster (a translucent white glass) were used for imitating semi-precious gems. Phoenician sailors carried these to India in a lucrative trade.

A rectangular white Egyptian glass rod, two inches long, inscribed in blue, was on display in the Imperial Museum in Berlin prior to World War I. It dates back to King Amenemet III (about 1830 B.C.). An engraved urn of blue glass (bearing the ring of the Pharaoh Thretmosis about 1700 B.C.) is lined in milk glass.

The Chinese made milk glass. Porcelain was supposedly invented in 185 B.C. When white, it is quite glassy; almost a milk glass. Glass pearls were manufactured under the Emperor Ou-ti in 140 B.C. The Chinese have been noted for their exquisite milk glass

through the centuries. Their vases and snuff bottles usually have applied patches of red or blue glass which are engraved or carved.

The Persians produced milk glass. The Caliph Omar (637 A.D.) had a magazine (large closet) which was lined with glass jars for drugs and spices. Milk glass jars and bottles were used for drugs for centuries after, in pharmacies.

Mosaics which have been highly prized for many centuries were made in Egypt during the Ptolemaic Period 323 B.C. to 30 B.C. In most of these tiny inlaid tiles, milk glass played a part. They are in the murals of many old churches and palaces. During the first century B.C. applied mosaics, large and small, lined the walls of Roman baths. Excavations at Pompeii have brought exquisite plaques to light. Specimens of ancient mosaics may be seen in the Metropolitan Museum of Art in New York City and in the Toledo Museum.

The finest product of milk glass of all history, is the famous Portland Vase in the British Museum. This was found in the Barberini tomb in Rome and dates back to the first century A.D. It is about a foot high, made of dark cobalt-blue glass, and bears applied milk glass parts which display engraving beauty almost beyond belief. After World War I, the Portland family, in need of funds, removed the Vase from the British Museum and placed it on auction at Christy's in London. It has been smashed by a demented visitor to the Museum, but repaired. The highest bid, $143,000 was refused, so this most precious specimen of engraved milk glass in the entire World again reposes in the British Museum.

The Venetians used milk glass as fibers or veins in their beautiful filigree plates, bowls and vases. They are now the white threads more commonly seen in twisted spirals of stems of wine glasses. Filigree was later produced in Bohemia (now Czechoslovakia). Milk glass was long ago first used as a lining or overlay in cased glasses. When the outer layer is cut or engraved the inner layer shows through in particularly attractive contrast. Some American producers have done and still do such work.

The story is sometimes told of a glass blower who fell into a melting furnace and thus helped produce the first milk glass from the phosphate in his bones. In early milk glass bone ashes were used! In the sixteenth century oxides of arsenic and tin were used. Now we employ fluorides, aluminum compounds, titanium oxide and other chemicals to produce modern "milkglass."

In 1830 Peruzzi started the manufacture of artificial glass eyes using milk glass. In 1621 the thermometer appeared under the name of Cornelius van Drebbel of Holland. Of course every thermometer has a Milk Glass layer so that we may easily see the height of the mercury or colored liquid column.

And now let us consider the first industrial enterprise in the American colonies, a factory located about a mile from Olde Jamestowne, in the Colony of Virginia, in 1609. Here bottles and/or beads were all supposedly made by Poles and Germans brought over by the London Company. The beads were to include white and turquoise varieties, plain and striped. They were to be used as currency for trade with the Indians; in other words, milk glass may have been a medium of exchange in our country long before American went on, and then off, the "gold standard."

Currently, the best-known American producers of hand-made glassware, banded together as Glass Crafts of America, are engaged with the U. S. National Parks Service in an effort to develop and restore Jamestowne's Old Glasshouse Point, already discovered, and will some day reveal to the general public that first industry of America, in all its romantic and historical glory! Perhaps added milk glass facts of importance will then come to light.

The general story of American milk glass is well known to most individuals. It is the story of milk glass vases, pitchers, glasses, bowls, lighting globes and reflectors, bath-room and kitchen tiles, plate glass walls, etc., made in a number of factories in America. It is believed that its firm American popularity first became readily noticeable in the 1870's. Many volumes on American pressed, blown and rolled milk glass have been written. However, the older backgrounds are not so well known. It is hoped these brief historical items, on earliest milk glass as here related, may prove of great interest to milk glass collectors and users everywhere, and Imperial Glass has had them especially developed, by competent authority, for your enjoyment and pleasure.[1]

Imperial Milk Glass

In 1950, when Imperial Glass Corporation began a new drive into the production of milk glass, the company began using "molds as old as fifty years in some instances, and from many of much more recent vintage. Imperial is producing by olden-day methods, Milk Glass of interesting shapes, designs, proper color and by skilled hands."[2]

As noted previously, a 1930s Imperial catalog pictured thirty pieces of opal glass. Early production was called opal glass rather than milk glass and was more translucent than the milk glass that we know from the 1950s production. According to the 1932 price list we have, Imperial produced twenty-four pieces in opal that year. As Imperial did, we like to describe the early milk glass as skim milk and the glass produced after 1950 as whole or homogenized milk. In 1950, the company noted the following about their milk glass production:

> Colored glasses have been known historically, far longer than has our most popular medium today—crystal glass. It is safe to assume that milk glass is almost as old as the art of glassmaking. It was probably first produced in America in New England, but certainly to the largest extent in the Pittsburgh area during the last one hundred years. You might be interested to know that molten evidence on refractory parts recently dug up at Jamestown, Virginia, seem to indicate that a type of milk glass was made down there as early as 1608.

> Our 1950 line of Vintage Milk Glass is of proper color. In past years we have had color trouble, but we notice through research and close study that even Westmoreland has had this difficulty—and we refer to them respectfully as the leaders in the milk glass field. Their color has moved through blues and creams and other tints from time to time, even during periods of consistent, steady manufacturing. We believe our new color can be held consistent through continuous production. We will carefully guard ourselves to keep from shipping unsatisfactory color.

> We believe we are the first to <u>deliberately</u> design some new items in milk glass. You will recognize many

of these as never having seen them before, even as antiques. We have resurrected some forty-year old molds from which to make other items. We are in the milk glass business to stay. Again let us reemphasize the fact that milk glass is the greatest portion of American women's first hobby—the collection of American made glass. We have deliberately tried not to copy items that exist on the market, and have thus presented a group we believe is susceptible to high collector interest.

> Milk glass popularity is now at its highest level! The 1949 release of a book, "Milk Glass" by E.M. Belknap, America's greatest authority on and largest collector of milk glass, has given new emphasis to interest and attention on this merchandise.[3]

The information for this book has been taken from many catalogs, price lists, memorandums, and written excerpts of the Imperial Glass Corporation. Early records and catalogs for the Imperial Glass Company are very scarce. Besides the 1930s Imperial catalog showing opal glass, we have price lists dated 1932, 1943, and 1950 (when Imperial set about to capture the milk glass market). Between 1950 and 1984 we have twenty-six catalogs and price lists on which to base the information presented in this book. In a 1952 catalog, the company wrote:

> There has never been produced a better Milk Glass color than in Imperial's Vintage line. Milk Glass, to be properly and readily acceptable, should have a milk white color—not skimmed milk or bluish-tinges—but the color of whole milk, with a slight rich, creamish accent. Much is called Milk Glass today which has a gray cast, and we too often hear opaque glass items in caramel, purple, green, ivory, blue, black, yellow, being called colored Milk Glass. Milk Glass cannot be other than the color of milk![4]

In their 1951 pamphlet on *The Story of Hand-Made Milk Glass*, the company had previously noted:

At Imperial, a conscientious effort is made, at all times, to produce Milk Glass items not made by other existing factories, and also, in marketing, every precaution is taken to keep this merchandise from being foisted upon the unenlightened as "antiques."[5]

Imperial did produce beautiful white milk glass. However, any factory will experience an occasional problem with a color they are making. Collectors will find milk glass that is not the desired white color. We doubt that Imperial shipped an inferior quality of color to its customers. Seconds were sold through its outlet shop, the Hay Shed. It is likely also that factory workers took some pieces with an undesirable tint home. Eventually many of these items found their way into the mainstream and the marketplace. This may account for the milk glass pieces found in an off white color. Occasionally, one appears with a smoke or very light violet tinge.

Imperial's regular milk glass finish, so well known, is a plain, glossy surface. Imperial also produced a unique finish on milk glass called Doeskin:

Our original and new "DOESKIN FINISH" is an Imperial process, and the words are an Imperial owned, registered trade-mark. This finish was inspired by Imperial's Cathay finish [c.1949], a study of alabaster, salt-glaze, suede, frosted, blasted and acideaten finishes formerly applied to glass by Imperial or other glass producers of modern or olden days, and by earthen-ware, pottery, crockery, stoneware and china makers over hundreds of years. Doeskin is the product of research, historical and modern, of science and Imperial's effort. It is different. Examination by prominent buyers of milk glass prior to January 1, 1950, at Imperial's factory, leads to the prophecy here and now made, that this finish is exciting, new, worthwhile and will give the milk glass picture the shot-in-the-arm it has needed for 100 years. How we do it is our trade secret until our application for method patent clears through its initial stages.[6]

In catalogs "B" and "C", Imperial also described Doeskin as "Imperial's original and exclusive Doeskin bisque-like alabaster-appearing surface."[7] Lucile Kennedy, former Assistant to the President, shared with us the following story about the beginning of Doeskin. An item of milk glass was brought to her with a finish similar to one of sand blasting. When asked what she thought about it, she replied that "it was beautiful," but she did not like to touch it. It had not yet been fire polished. It was explained to her that a number of milk glass pieces were made that had black (iron) flakes in them. A method of covering the flecks was sought in order to have a marketable product. Lucile added that after the item was fire polished, "it had the soft feel of Doeskin." It added to the cost of an item to apply a Doeskin finish, but it saved an item that would not have been acceptable. All Doeskin sold at a higher price than the regular finish and soon became a popular item.

This photo shows how the same item (#282 Americana Jar in Midwest Custard) looks with Imperial's Doeskin finish (on the right) compared with the regular, glossy finish (on the left).

Early Imperial catalogs and the 1932 and 1943 price lists use the prefix 11/ for the milk glass items produced. In 1950, the prefix was changed to 1950/ for the glossy milk glass and 1952/ for the Doeskin finish. Starting with the 1950 production, almost the entire line of milk glass was made in both the 1950/ glossy finish, and the 1952/ Doeskin finish. To simplify reading, we will only use the 1950/ prefix in this book. The exceptions to this dual production will be noted in the catalog illustration sections and the price list.

In our earlier research, it was always felt that the prefix 1950/ might indicate the year that Imperial began producing their enlarged line of milk glass. Imperial collectors at one time thought that the superimposed IG mark began with the 1950/ milk glass prefix. In researching this material for our first milk glass book, we learned that the 1950/ milk glass prefix did indeed begin in 1950, and as we all now know, the IG mark began in 1951. That explains why collectors have found so many unmarked pieces of milk glass known to be of the 1950 date. There was a time when we thought that 1952/ as a prefix for Doeskin might indicate the year that treatment began. However, our research for our first book clearly showed that Doeskin, too, began in 1950.

Placing a mark in a mold by glass companies was not always accomplished before a mold was put into use for reissue of an item. Often this omission could be an oversight. Other times it could happen if time was a factor—placing a new mark in a mold was both costly and time consuming. Imperial wrote in 1951:

> By important popular request, Imperial's Milk Glass "hallmark" [IG] (trademarked and copyrighted) as here shown beside these words, identifies each genuine piece of Imperial Vintage Milk Glass produced after February 1, 1951. So located as to not interfere with design attractiveness, this "hallmark" will always prove approximate age, identity and source, signify to quality and skilled hand craftsmanship, attest to sincere and talented design effort and add to the value of each item![8]

As an aid to readers, this book will include pattern names after the mold numbers when there is an appropriate name. Most names are company names, but "Candlewick," "Lace Edge Cut," "Leaf," and "Leaf Open" are descriptive names we have assigned for clarification purposes. Candlewick is not Imperial's name for the milk glass with beaded edge and raised flower design. We use the name "Candlewick" because of the beaded edge that is like the general 400/ line of Candlewick. When we use a name that we have assigned for identification, it will appear in quotation marks. According to information provided to us by a former Imperial employee when we were writing the first version of this book, the pattern that we list as "Leaf" was also known as Holly Leaf at the Imperial factory. In years past, that same pattern was erroneously called Star Holly.

When studying Imperial's milk glass, collectors should pay particular attention to the density of the glass. As noted above, the early milk glass, pre-1950, is somewhat translucent and is known as "skim milk." The later glass, from 1950 to the end, is known as "whole milk." Another distinction lies in the design. Some pieces of early milk glass stems have an intaglio design on the bottom side of the foot (intaglio is an incised figure below the surface of the material, so that an impression from the design yields an image in relief). Later milk glass stems will have a plain or stipple design. These pieces are examples of intaglio design: 11/473C 6" Compote, Grape; 11/4732B (1950/21) 6" Vase, Grape; and the (1950/473) 3 oz. Wine, Grape.

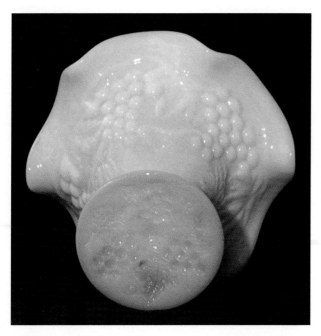

Intaglio design on the foot of the 11/473C Compote. This is an example of the design found on many of the pre-1950 milk glass pieces.

Part II

Decorations and Variations

Belknap Collection

A 1955 advertising folder gives this informative message: "Exclusive, accurate reproductions for the famous [E. McKamly] Belknap Collection, Early American Antique Milk Glass. Authorities recognize these treasures as the largest and most renowned private collection of Early American Milk Glass. We at Imperial are indeed proud that we have been granted exclusive permission to reproduce authentic replicas."[9]

The first piece of this collection appeared in 1951 and all of the twenty-one items were available from 1955 to 1958. All were discontinued by 1968. The 1950/330 was available again in 1977-1978. Listed next are the items from the Belknap Collection with first and last year dates of production.

1950/125	Wedding Bowl and Cover, Scroll	1953-61
1950/155	Rabbit-On-Nest	1953-58
1950/180	7 1/2" Vase, Grape	1955-68
1950/181	6 1/4" Vase, Rose	1955-68
1950/192	8 1/2" Tricorn Vase	1951-58
1950/194	9 1/4" Celery Vase	1952-60
1950/203D	10" Cake Stand, Open Edge	1955-60
1950/203F	8 1/2" Fruit Bowl, Open Edge	1955-64
1950/228	4-Toed Sugar and Cream, Both Covered	1955-60
1950/232	Oval Sugar and Cream, Both Covered	1955-60
1950/235	8" Berry Bowl, Scroll	1955-60
1950/236	5" Nappy, Scroll	1955-60
1950/267	Salz and Pfeffer Set	1955-60
1950/306	1 Quart Pitcher, Grape	1955-62
1950/307	6 oz. Footed Tumbler, Grape	1955-62
1950/321	60 oz. Pitcher, Scroll	1955-60
1950/322	12 oz. Tumbler, Scroll	1955-60
1950/325	3 1/4" Candleholder	1955-62
1950/330	7" Tall Candleholder	1955-60; 1977-78
1950/335	Owl Sugar and Cream	1955-60
1950/800	Owl Jar and Cover	1955-60

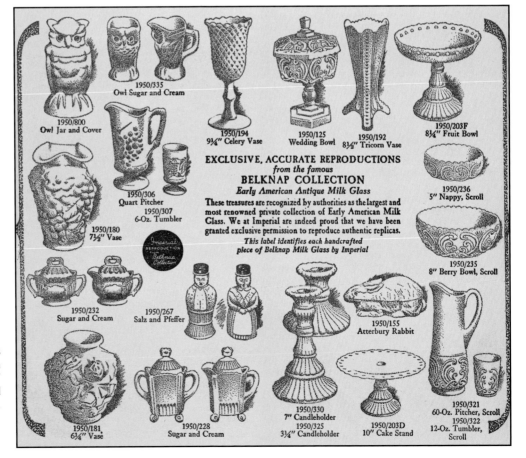

"Exclusive, Accurate Reproductions from the famous Belknap Collection Early American Antique Milk Glass." Original brochure from Imperial Glass Corporation c. 1951.

Atterbury Molds

"Thomas B. Atterbury was the outstanding glass designer of his times and many of his best articles were protected by early U.S. Patents," notes a 1957 tag for Imperial's Atterbury items. "He was operating two factories at capacity in the late 1880s and produced primarily Milk Glass and other Opaque glass. Atterbury originals are rare and seldom 'discovered' today. From the famed Belknap Collection, Imperial franchised permission to authentically reproduce many genuine Atterbury items of 1880-1890. Animals, birds and other fowl, bowls, scroll patterned tableware and accessory pieces, compotes, candleholders, open lace edged pieces are but a few among Imperial's many carefully-crafted handpressed Atterbury reproductions."[10]

The 1950/159 Atterbury Lion Box and Cover, 1950/159/1 Atterbury Bowl, 1950/214 Atterbury Dove Box and Cover, 1950/155 Rabbit-on-Nest, and 1950/800 Owl Jar and Cover are the items attributed to Mr. Atterbury. It is possible that other items could be attributed to Atterbury, but we have listed only those which were documented in the Imperial records.

1950/159 Atterbury Lion Box and Cover. $225-250.

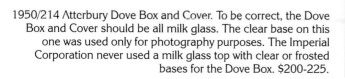

1950/214 Atterbury Dove Box and Cover. To be correct, the Dove Box and Cover should be all milk glass. The clear base on this one was used only for photography purposes. The Imperial Corporation never used a milk glass top with clear or frosted bases for the Dove Box. $200-225.

"Famous Atterbury Designs (Circa 1880)" POPA Tag. An Imperial Point of Purchase Aid was often attached to Imperial's products to give a customer information when making a purchase. Imperial referred to the POPA Tags as "Silent Salesmen always on the job." The inside reads:

"Thomas B. Atterbury of Pittsburgh was the outstanding Glass Designer of his time and many of his best articles were protected by early U.S. Patents. His Atterbury Company was operating two factories at capacity in the late 1880s producing what Historians of the Industry describe as 'FANCIES', as well as regular Patterned Tableware. Mr. Atterbury had 'the touch of artistry' and the ability to construct and operate Press Moulds which TRULY translated his deft designs into glass—primarily Milk Glass and other Opaque 'metals'. His primary Manufactory held to 'open pot' wood-fueled Melting far after most others had abandoned this type 'vessel' and method for 'hooded' pots and Coal Fire heat."

"Atterbury 'originals' are rare and seldom 'discovered' today. From the famed Belknap Collection, Imperial has franchised permission to authentically reproduce many Genuine Atterbury Items of 1880-90. This article is but one of them. Animals, Birds and other Fowl, Bowls, Scroll Patterned Tableware and Accessory Pieces, Compotes, Candleholders, Open Lace edged pieces are but a few among Imperial's many carefully-crafted Handpressed Atterbury Reproductions. If you are hunting for Heritage or searching for 'story'—these proud Atterbury Replicas will give enduring pleasure and bring welcome relief from the prosaic."

1950/800 Owl Jar and Cover. The original Atterbury Owl Jar and Cover had interlocking lugs to hold the top in place. The Imperial Owl Jar and Cover does not have the locking lugs. $80-85.

Hand Decorated—1950s

In addition to the milk glass items introduced in 1950, many hand decorated milk glass pieces were also introduced. Some of these special treatments are missing from our collection, so imagination will have to guide a collector in knowing what they look like.

The following six groups of information were taken from a 1950 Imperial memorandum:

> These pieces "are hand-decorated with enamels, with transparent colors and with metals. All pieces are fired. Some are on plain [glossy] Vintage surface milk and some on the Doeskin surface. The proper adjective is "beautility" . . . Be attentive to the Hobby Horse Cigarette Box and the Heart Set. They are our first attempt to do "peasant" or Berk's-County-Pennsylvania-Dutch types of hand decoration."[11]

Some of the following decorations are self-explanatory. Please remember that this is the only list we had about these six groups of decorated milk glass. We do not know how long the production continued but it seemed limited.

Gold Encrusted Band on Doeskin Finish

Only Doeskin finish is included in this group.

1952/525	10 1/2" Buffet Or Wall Plate, Homestead
1952/524	10 1/2" Buffet Or Wall Plate, Mum
1952/7D	9" Wall Or Luncheon Plate, Windmill

Decorated "Polychrome" on Doeskin Finish

Note that this decoration is on the Doeskin finish as well. We have seen these pieces and the paint is a vivid bright color. On the 1952/161 Covered Butter, the roses are a bright yellow. At the time we saw it, we doubted it was done at the factory. However, the 1950 Imperial memorandum noted above proves that this decoration is a factory product.

1952/10D	10 1/2" Wall Or Buffet Plate, Rose
1952/6D	9 1/2" Wall Or Luncheon Plate, Rose
1952/2526	Sugar and Cream Set, Family Reunion, Rose
1952/161	8" Covered Butter Or Cheese, Rose
1952/249	9 Piece Water Set, Rose

Hand-painted Colonial Rose

1950/23	3 Piece Mayonnaise Set, Open Border
1950/75D	11" Buffet Or Wall Plate, "Candlewick"
1950/75H	9" Heart Fruit Or Dessert Bowl, "Candlewick"
1950/75F	11" Couped Apple Bowl, "Candlewick"
1950/45	5" Jelly Comporte, "Candlewick"
1950/??	5" Fruit Centre Comporte, Crimped (mold number undetermined)
1950/5D	8" Salad Or Wall Plate, Open Border
1950/23B	5 1/2" Cute Dessert, Open Border
1950/23D	7 1/2" Bread and Butter Plate, Open Border

1950/103, 10" Footed Fruit Bowl, "Candlewick," decorated with the Colonial Rose decoration. This is an example of an existing item that is not on the company listing. There are other known examples of the hand-decorated 1950/103. Note that the decoration, Colonial Rose, describes the hand-painted flower design and does not refer to a raised design in the mold. $110-125.

Of interest to Imperial Candlewick collectors is the information about the four items in this decorated line that have the beads around the edge. Collectors consider them to be "companions" to the Imperial Candlewick line. We believe that the mention of this in our book *Imperial's Vintage Milk Glass* is the first documentation of hand decorated pieces of milk glass with the beaded edge. We still have not been able to find the mold number for the 5" Fruit Centre Comporte, Crimped, mentioned on the previous page.

Hand-painted Gold Scroll And Rose Decoration

We think the rose decoration in this group is painted on the plain surface of the lid and perhaps on the sides of the box.

| 1950/191 | 8 1/2" Partitioned Cigarette, Boudoir/Desk Box |
| 1950/144 | 5" Covered Puff, Pin or Desk Box |

Pennsylvania Dutch—Peasant Art

| 1950/134 | Hobby Horse Cigarette Box |
| 1950/750 | 3 Piece Heart Tid Bit Or Ash Tray Set, "Candlewick" |

1950/134 Hobby Horse Cigarette Box. This is a rare piece and is sought by collectors of the older milk glass, as well as by Imperial milk glass collectors. The box is designed to hold a pack of regular size cigarettes. With constant use probably not many of these jewels have survived for fifty years. The 1950 catalog is the only time the Hobby Horse is pictured. Remember that it was produced in glossy milk glass with hand-painting. The Doeskin finish was issued without hand-painting. $*

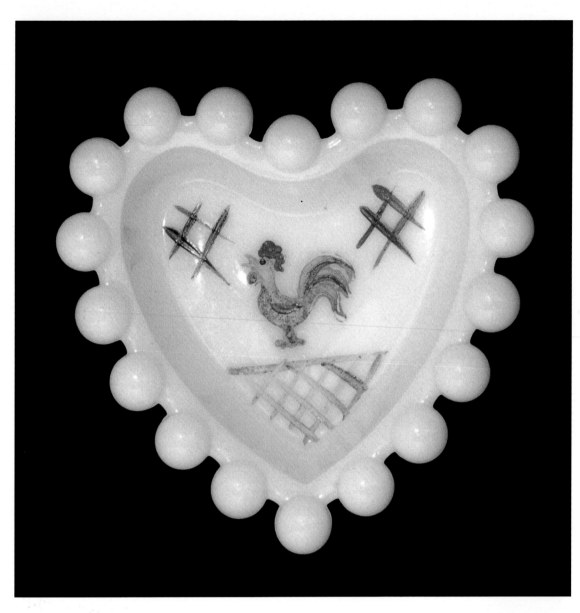

The 1950/750 Heart Tid Bit or Ash Tray Set is an exciting piece for Imperial Candlewick collectors. These milk glass pieces are made from Candlewick molds. They are hand-painted in Pennsylvania Dutch— Peasant Art. Most Candlewick collectors are not aware of this particular set. We were able to identify the painting on the heart by comparing the colors of paint and the decoration markings with the photo of the Hobby Horse in our first book, *Imperial's Vintage Milk Glass*. $35-45 each.

Miscellaneous

1950/60   5 1/2" Honey/Jam Decorated Gold Bees/Ribbon/Base
1950/79   11 1/2" 2 piece Hurricane Lamp, Crystal Chimney, Gold Scroll

1950/60 Honey or Jam Jar, decorated gold bees, ribbon, and base. $50-55.

Decorated Sugar and Cream Sets—1955

This is a hand-painted decoration, and from a study of catalog pictures showing Decorated Milk Glass Sugar and Creams (see next page), the "Ivy" seems to be decorated on the raised portion of the design. The "Dolly Madison," "Pansy," "Rose," and "Fruit" appear to have the decoration painted on the plain surface on the side of the sugar and cream.

1950/228/Dec	"Pansy" 4-Toed Sugar Cover and Cream
1950/232/Dec	"Rose" Covered Sugar and Cream
1950/348/Dec	"Dolly Madison" Sugar and Cream
1950/348/Dec	"Fruit" Sugar and Cream
1950/799/Dec	"Ivy" Sugar and Cream Set

1950/348/Decorated   "Dolly Madison"
Sugar and Cream Set

1950/348/Decorated   "Fruit"
Sugar and Cream Set

1950/799/Decorated   "Ivy"
Sugar and Cream Set

1950/228/Decorated   "Pansy"
4 Toed Sugar and Cream Set

1950/232/Decorated   "Rose"
Oval Sugar and Cream Set

Catalog C—Page 26

The decorated sugar and cream sets are seldom seen.
This factory catalog paper should help the collector to
identify the sets. $30-40 each set.

24

Decorated with Violets—1958-1959

This decoration is simply a purple violet, hand-painted and fired on the plain surface of these items.

1950/9/Dec	"Violet" Bundling Lamp
1950/232/Dec	"Violet" Covered Sugar and Cream
1950/456/Dec	"Violet" Handled Candy Box and Cover
1950/458/Dec	"Violet" Candy Box and Cover

Violet decorated milk glass items must be hard to find. In fact, we have never seen any of these pieces. Enjoy looking at this company photograph so that you will recognize this decoration. $*

Hand Decorated Concord Grape—1960s

In the early 1960s, Lotus Glass Company hand-painted several pieces of Imperial's Grape pattern. The leaves were a light green and the grapes were blue. The following is a list of the Lotus decorated pieces in light green and blue.

1950/6C	8" Crimped Bowl, Grape
1950/47C	9" Crimped Bowl, Grape
1950/191	Concord Ivy, Grape
1950/244	Handled Box and Cover, Grape
1950/468	4 1/2" Candy Jar and Cover, Grape
1950/471/3	3 Section Ivy Tower, Grape
1950/471/2	2 Section Ivy Tower, Grape
1950/735	Hex Candy Box and Cover, Grape
1950/810	Footed Candy Jar and Cover, Grape

In our collection is the 1950/471 3 Piece Ivy Tower. This is *not* the Ivy Tower described in the Lotus group, however: these leaves are dark green and the grapes are brown. We know of other grape items painted with green and brown as well. We are unsure of the story behind this painting, but our set did come from the Imperial factory area.

Lotus Glass Company is unique because it did not produce glass. They bought blanks from other glass companies and applied many types of decorations. Included in their decorations were hand-painting, cutting, etching, silver overlay, and applied gold. Adding to the confusion, Lotus Glass Company was located in Barnesville, Ohio, only about thirty miles from Imperial's location in Bellaire, Ohio. It remains undetermined if the set with the brown grapes is by an Imperial worker or is from Lotus. We tend to think that it was done by Imperial.

1950/471/3 Three Section Ivy Tower. This one is painted with green leaves and brown grapes and is *not* the documented Lotus decorated Ivy Tower. We believe this piece was decorated at the Imperial factory. $85-95.

Hand Decorated Coach Lamp Candy Jars—1958-1959

As noted in a 1958 advertising brochure, "The thirty-two sketches for the Dutch and Gay Nineties Jars are by Jane Snead, world known authority on these arts. Lynne Pepperdine did the sixteen Belles of 1890. Each of the four sides of each jar has a completely different sketch. Gay Ninety decorations are black, Pennsylvania Dutch designs are Olive and the Belles of 1890 are in Willow Ware Blue. Jars are 6 3/4" tall and 4 5/8" wide and are square. Jars and Covers are Genuine Handmade Milk Glass."[12]

Belles of 1890:	Coiffures
	Sports Femmes
	Fashions
	Millinery
Gay Nineties:	Bicycle Courtin'
	Skating In Central Park
	Bowery Cop Bar Jar
	Bein' Photographed
Pennsylvania Dutch Designs:	Spinning Wheel
	Courtin' Couple
	Market Day
	Newlywed's Farmhouse

1950/460/Dec, Pennsylvania Dutch Design; Newlyweds' Farmhouse. "Olive painted design and fired on the milk glass for lasting enjoyment." $*

Pennsylvania Dutch Designs

It has been recorded that as early as 1683 the German people began to arrive in Pennsylvania. Just a few years later there was also a large immigration from Switzerland. During a period of the next few years literally thousands of these people settled in the outskirts of Philadelphia, and before long the population grew to such an extent that the people soon spread out in the many counties of Pennsylvania and even into other states.

While the German immigration was prepondent over the Swiss, speaking much the same language, these people became what is today known as the Pennsylvania Dutch.

It is interesting to note, that even today, after a period of over two hundred years, the Pennsylvania Dutch speak with much the same dialect they had when first coming to this country.

Along with many other things the Pennsylvania Dutch brought with them their Art and used it as a decoration on whatever suited their tastes. They loved the simplicity of the flower motif, especially the tulip. Birds and animals of all description and, of course the human figure was extensively used. Many of their pieces were inscribed with names, dates and initials, which personalized their work and made it possible to detect the antiquity of some still existing today.

We are prone to think of the Pennsylvania Dutch Art as being crude but one could really say that it is the talent of an untrained hand that knew none of the rules of the schooled artist.

The designs being presented by Imperial Glass are an accumulation of Pennsylvania Dutch art work that I have collected over a period of the last ten years. Many are duplicates, as near as possible, of pieces I have seen in the museums, both in the east and the middle west. Others may be described as a stylized form of the same art.

In using these decorative Imperial pieces you will find perfect suitability and adaptability. The folk from whom we inherited these designs freely used such forms of decoration on their household articles such as pottery, tiles, furniture, linens, clothes and draperies.

Pennsylvania Dutch Art is very popular. People from all over the country are beginning to appreciate the lovely simplicity of it, for it is an art that anyone can understand.

My love for Pennsylvania Dutch folk lore comes naturally, for I am a direct descendant of these people through a family by the name of Pennypacker, which was my grandmother's maiden name.

Usually when one comes to the end of a project such as this, one heaves a sigh of relief, but I must admit that in this case I thoroughly enjoyed every minute spent on this art assignment for Imperial Glass Corporation. I sincerely hope your ownership of one or more of "my" four "Dutch" milk glass jars by Imperial will bring you pride and joy. Perhaps you'll also like "my" four "Gay Nineties" Coach Lamp Jars now offered by Imperial.

Sincerely,

Jane Snead

Imperial Glass Corporation advertisement for the
Pennsylvania Dutch Design by Jane Snead.

GAY NINETIES

The high tide of luxurious living swept America in that decade called the Naughty Nineties. Victorian prudery was the pretty screen for delightful cavorting. Get-rich-quick America was on a spree. We've all experienced nostalgic envy of grandparents' memories of the fantastic characters of this Gilded Age, the plush and plumes, the Nickel Beer with Free Lunch and the champagne-and-lobster living.

The waltz of the era WAS divine and Strauss was a living delight to the lovers of the day. Women were ladies and guys were gentlemen. Everything was gilded—storks brought the babies—beauties had a "Grecian bend" from whalebone and bustle—a kiss minus mustache was like an egg without salt—love-seats and portieres tempted all beaus.

Turrets and gables and baywindows decorated the homes where baths were warmed and taken in cozy kitchens. Foot-peddled reed organs were given as premiums for subscriptions to the Ladies Home Journal to make tunes in Horsehair furnished parlors as harmony came forth in great joy from tuneful voices singing "After the Ball," "On the Banks of the Wabash" and "Old Mill Stream." Klondike gold and Indian Lands made wealth for the bold and brazen.

Even the family life was romantic in these days of the Gilding of the Lily. Fine horses, stylish dogs and fancy Sleighs, Victorias and Surreys, Saloons and cloves, Beer Gardens and bicycle races, summer "Springs" vacations, torchlight parades for votes, strawberry festivals, horse cars, new "electric" trolleys, sparking, side-wheeler ships and boats with bar and "dealers" all added interest and "pace" to this era of the Gay Nineties.

Booth and Mantell, Sothern and Marlowe, Weber and Fields, Mrs. Fiske and the milk-bathing Anna Held starred in the Cast of this Age of sweet Innocence. The female shorthand writer was daringly new on the scene. Skating and dancing parties were the rage and couples "made time" on canal boat excursions and hayrides.

There was panic, Wall Street in crash, fraudulant railroads, business going smash, but the World's Fair was on and "without bread" all "ate cake" and laughed and were gleeful as they recited "Casey at the Bat." Morris chairs and Bloomer girls, Buffalo Bill and General Custer and the birth of the Imperial Glass Plant were all conversation provokers in these days. O, times of great events!

Today the Gay 90s comes to the living generation by stage, screen and television and through these Imperial Glass Corporation milk glass "Coach Lamp" Decorated Jars or Boxes. They are Imperial's and yours, exclusively. Jane Snead, nationally known artist and publisher has done the art for these fired decorations.

There are four separate and differently decorated Jars in this GAY NINETY series and another four by Mrs. Snead with Pennsylvania Dutch designs. Ask your favorite salesperson in your favorite store to show all of them to you.

The coach lamp shape of these multi-purpose items and the apt art on them, combine to give you a decorative, useful milk glass piece with bonus "conversational" value. There is a place and use for them in every room of every American Home! Wonderful for gift-giving!

Imperial Glass Corporation advertisement for the Gay Nineties by Jane Snead.

Next page:
Imperial Glass Corporation advertisement for the Pennsylvania Dutch Designs and Gay Nineties by Jane Snead. The Belles of 1890 are by Lynne Pepperdine.

BELLES OF 1890

Coiffures   Sports Femmes   Fashions   Millinery

GAY NINETIES

Bicycle Courtin'   Skating in Central Park   Bowery Cop Bar Jar   Bein' Photographed

PENNSYLVANIA DUTCH DESIGNS

Spinning Wheel   Courtin' Couple   Market Day   Newlyweds' Farmhouse

The thirty-two sketches for the Dutch and Gay Nineties Jars are by Jane Snead, world known authority on these arts. Lynne Pepperdine did the sixteen Belles of 1890. Each of the four sides of each jar has a completely different sketch: Gay Ninety decorations are Black, the Dutch ones are Olive and the Belles are in Willow Ware Blue. Jars are 6¾" tall and 4⅝" wide and are square. Jars and Covers are Genuine Handmade Milkglass.

Gold Flecked Milk Glass—1954-1957

Gold is applied mostly to the raised portions of the design but a small amount goes onto the background as well. It is "flecked," but much of the gold does touch, so it is not just applied in a splattered manner. The prefix 11/ specifies the decoration number rather than the early prefix (also 11/) used for opal glass dated before 1950.

Decoration	Description	Mold	Dates
11/108/Dec	6" Vase, Rose	1950/108	1954-57
11/191/Dec	Concord Ivy	1950/191	1954-57
11/486/Dec	8 1/2" Masque Vase	1950/486	1954-57
11/185/Dec	Fiddle Vase	1950/185	1954-55
11/186/Dec	Banjo Vase	1950/186	1954-55
11/143/Dec	6 1/2" Lovebird Vase	1950/143	1954-57
11/109/Dec	6" Vase Loganberry	1950/109	1954-57
11/192/Dec	8 1/2" Tricorn Vase	1950/192	1954-57
11/473/Dec	3 Pint Pitcher, Grape	1950/473	1954-57
11/356/Dec	10" Loganberry Vase	1950/356	1954-57
11/125/Dec	Wedding Bowl and Cover	1950/120	1954-57
11/120/Dec	Bridesmaid Bowl and Cover	1950/120	1954-56

Imperial Glass photograph showing the Gold Flecked items listed above.

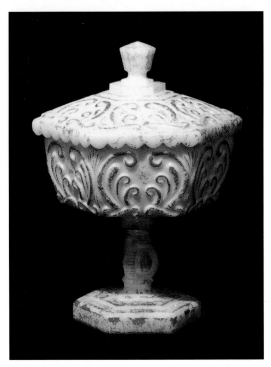

11/125/Dec, Gold Flecked
Wedding Bowl. $40-45.

11/185/Dec, Gold Flecked
Fiddle Vase. $35-40.

11/109 Dec, Gold
Flecked Loganberry
6" Vase. $35-40.

Antiqued Milk Glass—1961-1962

Unfortunately, we have no example of this. The word "Antiqued" suggests that the decoration is probably a burnished gold rather than a shiny gold. It should be easy to identify these pieces since you can tell by the listing that the antiqued decoration is applied to stems and a plate, not to the usual accessory pieces.

1950/3D	7 1/2" Plate, Grape
1950/473	10 oz. Goblet, Grape
1950/473	9 oz. Tumbler, Grape
1950/473	6 oz. Sherbet, Grape
1950/473	12 oz. Tumbler, Grape

Vigna Vetro Milk and Colored Glass Mixed—1959-1960

In 1959, Imperial wrote: "Vigna Vetro is Italian for Vineyard Glass and was first made by Briati in Italy then quickly copied at Nailsea in England. Sandwich played with it in this country. It has been termed as another Slag Glass but, of course, such is a partial misnomer for the colors in the milk metal could NEVER have been secured by use of iron. We [Imperial] make it in an entirely different manner than our PURPLE [slag] and also quite unlike our MURRHINA method. Great speed and skill is required but exact control is not possible, so once again, no two pieces can be alike."[13]

Murrhina, referenced in the above quotation, is a double cased glass and difficult to make. All shapes were hand formed. The crystal handles were hand-made and hand-stuck. Murrhina items are clear glass with suspended colors swirled throughout. Murrhina does have a bit of milk glass in with the other suspended colors.

We currently have two examples of Vigna Vetro, the 1950/180 and 1950/241. The colors blue, green, and yellow are speckled over the layer of milk glass—this is the way a non-glass maker might describe it. Because it is so different, a collector would certainly have to know what he or she was looking at to be aware at first glance that this was an Imperial milk glass item. Our pieces have drawn mixed comments. The most common one is, "I really like it . . . it is so different." We also hear humorous, negative comments.

1950/241 Vigna Vetro Cruet and Stopper, Grape. Note that the stopper is milk glass and not covered with the blue, green, and yellow particles. This is the correct stopper. $85-95.

1950/180 Vigna Vetro, 7 1/2" Vase, Grape. $30-35.

1950/163	Decanter and Stopper, Grape
1950/180	7 1/2" Vase, Grape
1950/310	Bud Vase, Grape
1950/241	Cruet and Stopper, Grape
1950/287	10" Vase, Grape
1950/356	10" Vase, Crimped Loganberry

Black Glass with Milk Glass Combination—1953-1955

This is a very striking combination of black glass and milk glass. It is another example you might pass by if you were not aware of it—unless you knew that Imperial deliberately put these black and milk glass pieces together, you would think it was a marriage of glass. The 419/ prefix is the decoration number assigned to this group.

419/59	5 1/2" Jar and Cover
419/60	5 1/2" Honey Jar and Cover, Gold Bees
419/120	Bridesmaid Bowl and Cover, Scroll
419/300	3 Piece Caster Set (Caster, Salt and Pepper)
419/420	14 Piece Tom and Jerry Set (Ladle, Bowl, and Cups), Grape
419/422	Atlantis Cigarette Box and Cover
419/450	4 Piece Trivet Set, 2 Black and 2 Milk Glass
419/4283	Basket With Salt and Pepper
419/8532	5 Piece Hors D'oeuvre Set (Tray/Pears), Grape

419/59 Jar and Cover, 5 1/2". $40-45.

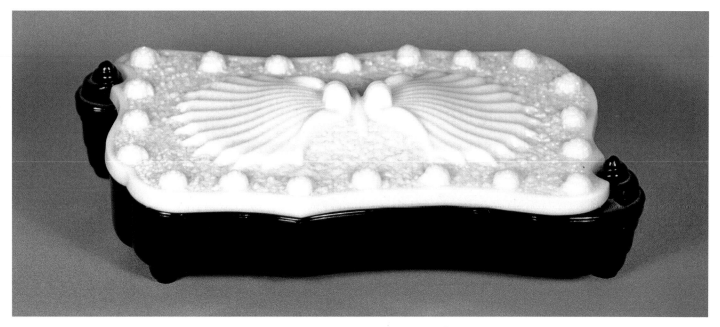

419/422 Atlantis Cigarette Box and Cover. $65-75.

35

1300 Reeded Perfume 3 Piece Set. This set has been found several times in different combinations. The combinations can be milk glass with black stoppers and lid, black bottles with white stoppers, all milk glass, and all black. This set is not documented in milk glass or the black and white combinations. $90-100.

Milk Glass and Metal—1953-1961

In the 1950s, Imperial combined milk glass with different types of metal. The metals used in the groups were brass, wrought iron, and cast iron. Often collectors of Imperial glass find a piece of glass combined with metal and think that another company bought the glass and made the combination. This they did often, but Imperial also combined glass and metal and marketed that item as a regular Imperial product.

Listed here are the pieces making up the Imperial groups. The numbers indicated are those used in the Imperial catalogs. B is for brass and W is for the Colonial Black Iron. The wrought iron items were simply numbered 1 through 7. For this special treatment, the company used the prefix number 1953 for regular milk glass and 1954 for Doeskin. When necessary, the Imperial milk glass mold number is added for clarity.

Study these groups carefully, because if the milk glass items are separated from the metal during an estate sale or similar sale, only the knowledgeable collector will know to look for the metal holder or frame.

Golden Brass and Milk Glass—1956-1958

The brass bases are fitted to the bottom of some items. Other items are placed into frames. The Golden Brass is similar to the size of the metal in the wrought iron.

B47C	10" Crimped Bowl, Grape
B62C	9" Crimped Bowl, Rose
B109	6" Vase, Loganberry
B111	6" Vase, Mum
B128	3 Piece Salad Set, Grape
B160	3 1/2" Candleholder, Rose
B191	Concord Ivy, Grape
B207C	7 1/2" Crimped Bowl, Lace Edge
B402	Cigarette Holder, Collectors Crystal
B473	3 Pint Pitcher (Vase), Grape
B1280	10 Piece Punch Set, Bowl, Brass Ladle, 8 Cups, Grape
B588	Sugar and Cream Set
B612	Salt and Pepper Set
B701	Cocktail Shaker, Reeded
B790	Sugar and Cream Set, Lace Edge

B880	3 1/2" Candleholder, Grape
B4733	3 Piece Marmalade Set, Grape
B12555	Lamp Swing (1950/114 Vase), Grape
B12556	Candelabra (1950/114 Vase) Grape
B12557	Labrette (1950/28C Vase)(1 Dozen Tiny Tapers)

B701 Reeded Cocktail Shaker, 11". The Reeded pattern is a large line in Imperial Glass. It has over thirty pieces in at least ten different colors. Reeded was introduced in the 1930s and continued occasionally until the 1960s. This is a little known pattern that makes a great collection. $90-100.

B402 Cigarette or Toothpick Holder. Imperial often gave different names to identical items during different time periods. Toothpick holders are enjoyable items to collect and can be found in many colors. $20-22.

Imperial photographs showing Golden Brass and Milk Glass
items. These items are listed on the previous page.

B111, 6" Vase, Mum. This vase can be found in many colors. $22-25.

B12555 Lamp Swing, Grape. $75-85.

Milk Glass in Wrought Iron Frames—1953-1956

These items were sold in regular milk glass as well as Doeskin with metal combinations. This is a combination that a collector might at first think was "put together." Imperial used similar wrought iron in combination with crystal Cape Cod. So far, few of these documented frames have been found. In forty-four years, probably most have been separated from the frames. The mat finished wrought iron and milk glass combinations appeared in Imperial records with a number 1 through 7.

#1 11 Piece Punch Set (1950/128 Bowl, 1950/4737 Cup), Grape
#2 Buffet Trio Server (2-1950/69, 1950/259 Bowl/Cover)
#3 Twin Jar Server (2 1950/94 Jar/Cover and Frame), Cape Cod
#4 Duo Shell Tid Bit (2 1950/297 Shell Tray and Frame)
#5 5 Piece Condiment Set (1950/247 Salt and Pepper, 2-1950/241 Cruet and Stopper and Frame), Grape
#6 Basket (1950/52C Crimped Bowl and Frame) Windmill
#7 Duo Mayonnaise Set (2 1950/723 Bowls, 2 1950/723 Black Ladle and Frame), "Leaf"

Imperial photo of #1, 11 Piece Punch Set (1950/128 Bowl, 1950/4737 Cup), Grape. $145-155.

#3 Twin Jar Server is sought by milk glass collectors as well as by Cape Cod collectors. $100-125.

#7 Duo Mayonnaise Set, Leaf. $65-75.

#5 Condiment Set, Grape. $50-60.

Colonial Black Iron and Milk Glass—1957-1961

Cast iron is what comes to mind when trying to think how to describe the colonial black iron sets. The W2 Lamp Stand Ivy set we found has the iron marked Wilton, but we have no proof that this company supplied the black iron to Imperial. The other holders do not have a marking on them. The 1950/152 and 1950/182 vases are not found in the regular milk glass catalogs and price lists. The W1 and W2 vases are the same shape as the 1950/114 Grape Lamp Vase. The 1950/152 and 1950/182 Vases have a simple small stippled or granular exterior.

W1	Wall Lamp Ivy	1950/152 Vase
W2	Lamp Stand Ivy	1950/152 Vase
W3	Eagle Planter	1950/182 Vase
W4	Lyre Planter	1950/182 Vase

1950/152 Lamp Vase. This vase has a lightly stippled effect on the bulbous bottom. It has no design on it and was used in the W1 and W2 Colonial Black Iron items. $40-45.

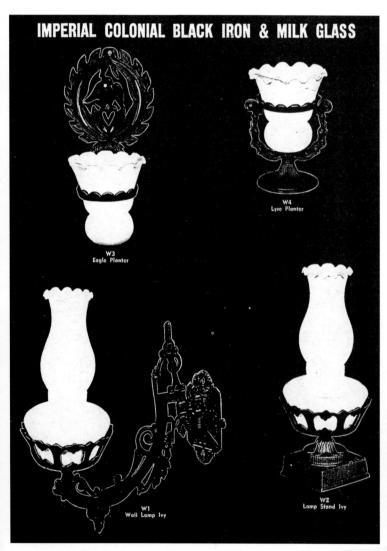

Imperial catalog page introducing a new promotion of the Colonial Black Iron items. Only a few of these have been found. $95-115.

Whirlspool Jars with Brass Knob and Cover—1956-1958

The Whirlspool Jar is from Imperial's Reeded line #701. It is shown in the company's 1930s catalog and is listed in a 1937 price list. This particular jar can be found in several colors. It was produced both with and without a knob. Additionally, we have seen chrome as well as brass knobs. Perhaps the jars came with chrome knobs also. We purchased replacement chrome knobs at the Hay Shed several years ago.

B702	5" Jar and Cover
B703	6" Jar and Cover
B704	7" Jar and Cover
B705	8" Jar and Cover
B7025	4 Piece Jar and Cover Set

B702 and B703 Reeded Jar and Cover with brass knobs. $25-30 each.

Opaque Glass—1955-1959

This book is dedicated primarily to milk glass. The many various and unusual treatments added to Imperial milk glass items are included here because they are of interest to Imperial collectors as well as milk glass collectors. You often hear glass collectors say "blue milk glass" or "black opaque." Logically, milk glass can only be the color of milk—white. Through the years, however, collectors began adding colored opaque glass and slag glass to their white opaque collections. The popularity of these other pieces among collectors is illustrated by the fact that the newsletter of the National Milk Glass Collector's Society is titled the *Opaque News*. Space does not allow for all illustrations and individual dates of the opaque and slag items, but this comprehensive list of the pieces that were produced should be a great help to collectors.

Forget-Me-Not Blue and Midwest Custard were introduced first (1955-1958) and Turquoise was added later (1956-1959). Using the following list, collectors can determine which opaque colors were available for each item. B is used for Forget-Me-Not Blue, C is for Midwest Custard, and T is for Turquoise. The addition of the D stands for Doeskin.

The 5002 and 5026 are from the Cathay line. The number 123 is Imperial's Chroma line; the four Chroma pieces (AKA Coronet, 1938; and Victorian, c. 1940s) are the Goblet, Sherbet, Footed Ice Tea, and 8" Plate. They were not shown in regular milk glass catalogs after the 1950s. The rest of the opaque items are from milk glass molds considered to be regular milk glass production items.

Mold	Description	Color Abbreviations
5D	8" Plate, Grape	B
28C	5" Whimsical Ivy	T, TD
59	5 1/2" Jar and Cover	T, TD
62C	9" Crimped Bowl, Rose	B, BD, C, CD, T, TD
67	8 1/2" Vinelf Compote	B, BD, C, CD, T, TD
73	5" Pansy Basket	T, TD
103	10" Footed Fruit Bowl, "Candlewick"	B, BD, C, CD, T, TD
109	6" Loganberry Vase	T, TD
116	6" Vase, Rose	B BD, C, CD, T, TD
123	Goblet, Chroma	C
123	Sherbet, Chroma	C
123	Footed Ice Tea, Chroma	C
123	8" Plate, Chroma	C
125	Footed Wedding Bowl/Cover, Scroll	B, BD, C, CD, T, TD
128	15 Piece Punch Set, Grape	T, TD
132	Urn, Dancing Nudes	B, C
147	4" Swan Mint Whimsy	T TD
160	3 1/2" Candleholder, Rose	B, BD, C, CD, T, TD
180	7 1/2" Vase Grape	B, BD, C, CD, T, TD
181	6 1/4" Vase, Rose	B, BD, C, CD, T, TD
274C	7" 4-Toed Compote, Lace Edge	T, TD
282	Americana Jar and Cover	B, BD, C, CD, T, TD
282/1	Jar and Cover	T, TD
322	11 oz. Goblet, Scroll	T
322	7 oz. Sherbet, Scroll	T
322	12 oz. Ice Tea, Scroll	T
322	8" Salad Plate, Scroll	T
356	10" Loganberry Vase	B, BD, C, CD, T, TD
422	Atlantis Cigarette Box and Cover	B, BD, C, CD
473	10 oz. Goblet, Grape	B
473	6 oz. Sherbet, Grape	B
473	12 oz. Ice Tea, Grape	B
474C	7" Compote	T, TD
727	Footed Candy Box and Cover, Grape	T, TD
743	Puff Box and Cover, Hobnail	B, BD, C, CD, T, TD
744	Cologne & Stopper Crimped, Hobnail	B, BD, C, CD, T, TD
745C	6" Crimped Bowl, Hobnail	T, TD
745F	6" Bowl, Lace Edge	T, TD
746	4 1/2" Vase, Hobnail	T, TD
778	7" Dolphin Comporte	B, C
893	Jar and Cover with Handle, Grape	T, TD
5002	Shang Jar and Cover, Cathay	B, BD, C, CD
5026	Phoenix Bowl, Cathay	B, C

#103 Footed Fruit Bowl, 10", "Candlewick." Forget-Me-Not Blue. $75-85.

#282 Americana Jar in glossy Midwest Custard on the left and Doeskin on the right. Both are seldom seen. $70-80.

#103 Interior View. Note that the Opaque #103 will have the vertical lines on the outer rim of the outside and the flower design on the inside. $75-85.

#893 Jar and Cover with Handle, Grape. Turquoise. $45-50.

#282 Americana Jar and Cover. Forget-Me-Not Blue, Midwest Custard, and Turquoise. $70-80 each.

#744 Cologne and Stopper, Crimped, Hobnail. Midwest Custard, Glossy. $40-45.

#744 Cologne and Stopper, Crimped, Hobnail. Turquoise, Doeskin. $40-45.

#181, 6 1/4" Vase, Rose. Midwest Custard, Glossy. $40-45.

#125 Footed Wedding Bowl, Scroll. Midwest Custard, Doeskin. $50-55.

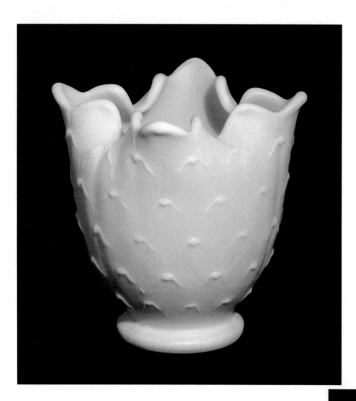

#28C, 5" Whimsical Ivy, Turquoise Doeskin. The Whimsical Ivy is made from the 1950/22 Pineapple Vase mold. The Pineapple Vase is one of the most easily found pieces of Imperial Milk Glass. Whimsical Ivy, Turquoise, $20-25.

#160, 3 1/2" Candleholder, Rose. Midwest Custard. $25-30 pair.

#116, 6" Vase, Rose. Forget-Me-Not Blue Iridescent. Documentation for the iridescent finish has not been found. $*

Black Glass

Several items of black Candlewick have been found. Since the publication of our first milk glass book in 1992, we have found paper documentation for the black Candlewick items listed below. The 3400 goblet was made in plain black (date unknown), while all others can be found with and without painted decoration. Most are decorated with a red, white, and gold stylized flower, painted and fired on decoration. These items were decorated at the factory and produced in 1937 for Butler Brothers Catalog sales. The decoration is named Cosmos.

400/74SC	9" 4-Toed Crimped Bowl
400/62D	8 1/2" 2 Handled Plate
400/62E	8 1/2" Plate with 2 Turned Up Handles
400/75N	7" 4-Toed Bowl
400/74B	8 1/2" 4-Toed Bowl
400/62EC	8 1/2" Bowl Turned Up Sides
3400	Goblet

Imperial produced other items in black during the 1930s. Some can be identified by the red, white, and gold stylized flowers similar to those found on the 1937 black Candlewick with Cosmos decoration.

Powder Box. Here is an example of the decorated black glass made by the Imperial Glass in the 1930s. $60-70.

400/62D, 8 1/2" Plate with the Cosmos Decoration, Candlewick. This was sold to Butler Brothers in the 1930s. $150-175.

Black Suede

In 1943, Black Suede was introduced by Imperial. This is a group that contained the Lalique Crystal Eagle and the Burnished Gold Glass Eagles. Since this same eagle produced in crystal was an addition to a Candleholder in the Candlewick and Cape Cod patterns, collectors of those patterns covet the eagles and hunt for the Crystal, Lalique, and Burnished Gold as well as the rare Milk Glass Eagle. Due to a conflict of trade names, the company dropped the Lalique term soon after using it in the 1940s. Satin, frosted, or acid etched would describe the finish.

L/777/3	Lalique Crystal Eagle Bookends with Two-Tone "Black Suede" Glass Base, 9" h.
G/777/3	Burnished Gold Glass Eagle Bookends with Gold Trimmed "Black Suede" Glass Base, 9" h.

L4/1943	Two-Tone "Black Suede" Glass Candy Jar With Cover, 7"
L4/1943	6 1/2" Pipe Bowl in Two-Tone "Black Suede" Glass
L4/1943	Tobacco Humidor Jar in Two-Tone "Black Suede" Glass
L4/1943	5 Piece Cigarette Set in Two-Tone "Black Suede" Glass. Mug Holder and 3 1/2" Ash Trays
L4/1943	Combination Cigarette Server and Ash Tray In "Black Suede" Glass, Holds 3 Smokes
L4/1776/1	3 Piece Cigarette Set in Two-Tone "Black Suede" Glass. Goblet Holder and 2 Eagle Ash Trays

Black Suede (prefix 4/) and Black and Gold (prefix 4/—/Dec Gold) were put back in the line in 1953. Most of the items were issued in both finishes. An asterisk next to the mold number indicates that the piece was made from a mold used for the general line of milk glass; the corresponding catalog illustration can be seen in the catalog illustrations beginning on page 76.

Mold	Description	Suede	Dec Gold
4/5022	Candy Box and Cover, Fan Shape, Cathay	X	X
4/5026	Phoenix, Cathay	X	
4/120 *	Bridesmaid Bowl and Cover, Scroll	X	X
4/80 *	7 1/2" Vinelf Candleholder	X	X
4/297 *	7 ½" Shell Tray		X
4/779 *	5" Dolphin Candleholder	X	X
4/108 *	6" Vase, Rose	X	X
4/109 *	6" Vase, Loganberry	X	X
4/143 *	6 1/2" Lovebird Vase	X	X
4/67 *	8 1/2" Vinelf Comporte	X	X
4/778 *	7" Dolphin Comporte	X	X
4/486 *	8 1/2" Masque Vase	X	X
4/356 *	10" Loganberry Vase Crimped	X	X

L4/1776 Eagle Ash Tray. $100-110.

L4/1943 Ashtray, $25-30.

Imperial made vases in a large variety of shapes and sizes—one could have a colossal collection of Imperial vases alone in various colors! Shown at right is the 4/108, 6" Vase, Rose; it is finished with the Black Suede treatment. The 4/109, 6" Loganberry Vase on the left is an example of the glossy black. Black is only one of many different colors used for this vase. $22-25 each.

Through the years, Imperial made items in black glass that were not necessarily part of a promotional effort. In the Cape Cod pattern there is a documented 1950/1602 Cigarette Lighter in black, made from 1962-1966. A 4-Piece Bridge set, #51885BK, was made from 1980-1981. This latter set was from the Heisey Puritan mold. A four piece Footed Salt Dip set, SD6, was also made in black from 1966-1969.

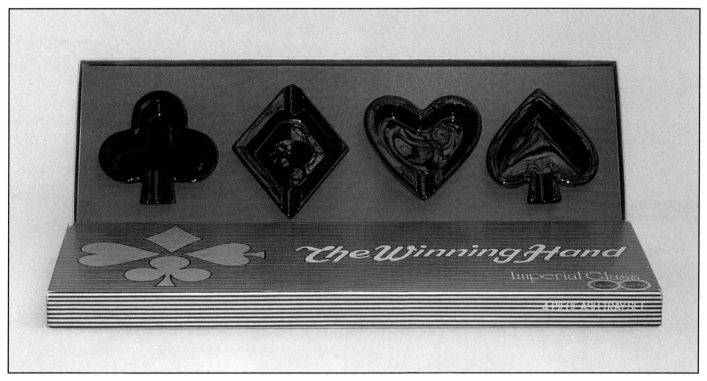

#51885BK 4-piece Bridge Set made in 1980-81 from the Heisey Puritan mold. $40-50.

Black Animals

The following animals in black were probably done on a feasibility basis; Imperial occasionally made a limited number of an item to study and decide if it should be added to the general line. We have seen these animals, but we do not have documentation or dates.

Scotty
Bull
Cygnet
Mallard Wings Down
Standing Colt
Kicking Colt

These black animals were offered for sale in 1980:

Tiger Paperweight
Airedale
Donkey
Elephant
Gazelle
Pig
Scolding Bird

49

Slag Glass

According to literature from Imperial, "Slag Glass or End O'day Glass is a years-old, original creation of the glassworkers themselves, who at the end of a work day, would combine milk glass with a colored glass to produce the unique 'marble effect.' No two pieces of slag glass are alike, and each reflects the individuality of the glassworker. Imperial creates Jade Slag—shades of turquoise green with white milk glass; Caramel Slag—deep rich caramel hues with traditional milk glass; and Ruby Slag, the ultimate in slag glass—combines bright ruby glass with milk glass. The vibrant reds and fiery colors are created by reheating the item after it is hand formed."[14]

Not to be confused with what is called Marble Glass or End-of-Day Glass, Imperial's Slag Glass is a "purposefully deliberate, distinctive and carefully-produced separate, Unusual Glass."[15] Oddly, the Imperial catalogs and price guides do refer to Ruby Slag as "End O' Day."

Frosting was one of the techniques used in the production of slag glass: "Glass, such as Imperial's Slag line, is frosted by sand blasting. The sand blasting process consists of spraying an abrasive material, such as sand, onto the surface of the glass at high pressure and great speed. A glass article can be frosted all over by sand blasting to a silky satin finish or to a deep rough finish, depending on the time of exposure to the blast of sand and the coarseness of the sand blasting material."[16]

The number of items produced in the various slags ran from a low of nine Purple Slag items in 1959 to a high of forty-four Caramel Slag items in 1970, with over one hundred different items made in slag between 1959 and 1977. Slag was issued in glossy and satin for most of the items but not all. The largest exception to this is that the Caramel Slag animals were made in glossy only. Years of production for the different colors are as follows:

Purple Slag	1959-1975
Caramel Slag	1965-1977; 1982-1982
Ruby Slag	1969-1977
Jade Slag	1975-1977

The items below were produced in various colors of slag between 1959 and 1977. In 1982, twenty-six pieces were made again in Caramel Slag. Note that the first numbers are the mold numbers of the slag line and do not always reflect the milk glass numbers. Slag is a story by itself and space does not allow for full illustration of all the items.

The items marked with an asterisk are made from molds used for milk glass items (see catalog illustrations beginning on page 76). The five-digit number after the description is the Lenox computer number used after 1973. It is given as an aid for collectors who may have a catalog for reference dated after 1973.

Number	Description	Lenox Number	Slag Color
1	Cask Bottle and Clear Stopper		P
1	Tooth Pick Holder	43620	R
9 *	Bundling Lamp		P
9/1	4" Nut or Mint		P
19	Footed Toothpick Holder	43630	P, C, J
30 *	Sugar and Cream Set, Lace Edge		C
40 *	9 1/2" Basket, Daisy	43644	P, C
46	12 oz.. Goblet		P
47C *	9" Crimped Bowl, Grape		R
48 *	7" Compote		C
52C *	8" Crimped Bowl, Windmill		C
60 *	5 1/2" Covered Honey Jar	43906	P, C, J
61	Salt Dip		R
62C *	9" Crimped Bowl, Rose	43699	P, C, R, J
74C	8" 3-Toed Bowl, Rose	43693	P, C, J
78	Footed Bowl and Cover		C
81	5" Handled Candleholder		P
98	10" Cake Stand		P
104 *	Miniature Pitcher	43636	P, C, J
123	3" Cornucopia	43528	P, C, R, J
132 *	8 1/2" Urn, Dancing Nudes		R
133 *	Covered Jar		C
133/1	6" Vase		C
146 *	4 1/2" Duck-On-Nest	43920	P, C, J
147 *	4" Swan Mint Whimsy	43930	P, C, J
150 *	5" Ash Tray, Feather		P
154	Eagle Mug		R
156 *	5 1/2" Basket/Milk Glass Handle	43642	P, C, R, J
156 *	Box and Cover		P, C, R, J

No.	Description	Mold	Colors
157 *	Rabbit Box and Cover		P
158 *	Rooster Box and Cover	43870	P, C, J
159 *	Lion Box and Cover		P, C
159/1 *	7 1/4" Bowl, Atterbury		P
160 *	3 1/2" Candleholder, Rose	43784	P, C, R, J
176 *	4-Toed Jar and Cover	43882	P, C, R, J
191 *	Partitioned Covered Box		P
191/150	3 Piece Cigarette Set		P
192 *	8 1/2" Tricorn Vase	43762	P, C, R, J
194 *	9 1/2" Celery Vase		C
199 *	Shell Tray	43580	C
203F	8 1/4" Footed Bowl		P
210 *	Robin Shaving Mug, Peanut Jar	43325	P, C, R
210/1 *	Flower Arranger, Frog		P
240 *	1 Pint Pitcher, Windmill	43150	P, C, R, J
274c *	7" 4-Toed Compote, Lace Edge		P
284	Swung Vase (Height 11" to 14")		R
291 *	4 1/2" Atlantis Shell Ash Tray		P
294 *	4 1/2" Heart Ash Tray	43854	R
297 *	7 1/2" Shell Tray		C
300	9 1/2" Tall Basket		R
312 *	Heart Leaf Covered Box		P
312/1 *	Heart Bowl, Tray, Server		P
330	7" Tall Candleholder		P
332	10 and 12 oz. Tumblers, Scroll		C
335 *	"Owl" Sugar and Cream Set	43540	P, C, R, J
352	7 3/8" Candleholder		P, C
363F *	6" Bowl, "Lace Edge, Cut"		P
377 *	Covered Pie Wagon	43890	C
400	8" Swan	43932	P, C, J
413 *	10 oz. Tumbler, Grape		C
431C	6 1/2" Tall Crimped Compote		R
456	7 1/2" Handled Candy Box and Cover		P
459 *	Rooster Holder	43639	C, R, J
461 *	"Eagle" Covered Footed Box		P, C
464	Pokal	43910	P, C, R, J
473 *	10 oz. Tumbler, Grape	43060	R
475 *	5 1/2" Basket		R
478	5 1/2" Handled Nappy	43574	C, R, J
505 *	Toothpick Holder	43624	P, C, J
505 *	Cruet and Stopper	43490	P, C, J
514	Minuet Girl	43835	C
524	10 3/4" Plate, Windmill	43401	C
529	10" Footed Vase	43770	C, R, J
552	11 oz. Goblet (No Design)		C
552	5 1/2 oz. Wine (No Design)		C
552	5 oz. Sherbet (No Design)		C
552	11 oz. Tumbler (No Design)		C
588	Sugar and Cream		P
593	Goblet, 8 1/2 oz. Panel		P
602	6" Bowl, Lace Edge		C
602	11" Bowl, Lace Edge		C
611	Box and Cover		P, C, J
613	Vase	43759	C
640 *	4 1/2" Nappy, Hobnail		P
641 *	8 1/2" Bowl, Hobnail		P
642	10" Bowl, Hobnail	51700	P
661	5" Vase	43752	P, C, J
666	Vase Panel Sides	43763	C
666	Sugar and Cream	43530	C
671	Candlestick	43794	C
702	7 1/2" Apothecary Jar and Cover		P
704	9 1/2" Apothecary Jar and Cover		P
720	Bell	43842	P, C, R, J
727C	4" Footed Compote	43723	P, C, J
737A	8 1/2" Footed Bowl	43698	P, C, R
747C	Footed Compote		C
759	Box and Cover	43876	R
761	Compote		C
778 *	7" Dolphin Compote		C
779 *	5" Dolphin Candleholder		C
780 *	6" Covered Bowl, Lace Edge		P
780 *	14 Piece Punch Set, Lace Edge		P
800 *	Owl Jar and Cover	43900	P, C, J
821	Box and Cover, Squirrel		P
822	Box and Cover, Dog	43199	P, C
823	Box and Cover, Duck		P
825	Box and Cover, Bee		P
851 *	5" Handled Nappy, Grape	43576	R
860 *	Footed Bowl and Cover, 9 1/2" Tall		C
880 *	3 1/2" Candleholder, Grape		R
965	10" Footed Vase, Pinched Neck		R
971	Flat Iron Box and Cover		P
973	6 1/4" Compote		P
981 *	Olden Pitcher, Vase		P
1123	Dresden Girl Bell	43846	C
1489	4 1/2" Square Ash Tray		P
1519/45	Footed Oval Compote		C
1519/59	Covered Candy		C
1519/140	Footed Jar and Cover		C
1560	Box and Cover	43897	P, C, R, J
1591 *	Storybook Mug	43320	C, R, J
1602 *	Cigarette Lighter Cape Cod		P
1605	7 1/2" Bowl	43681	C, R, J
1608/1	7" Ash Tray, Square	43858	P, C, R, J
1776 *	Eagle Holder	43240	R
1956	8" Ash Tray, Hambone	43865	P, C, R, J
2006	Dolphin Candy Box and Cover		P
5930	6" Compote	43729	P, C, J
6007	36 oz. Pitcher	43154	C
6992	Box, Beaded Edge and Cover		P, C

/156 Basket, 5 1/2", Ruby Slag. $55-60.

/158 "Rooster" Box
and Cover, Jade Slag.
$175-200.

/335 "Owl" Sugar and
Cream Set, Ruby Slag.
$70-80.

/459 Rooster Holder, Ruby Slag. $50-60.

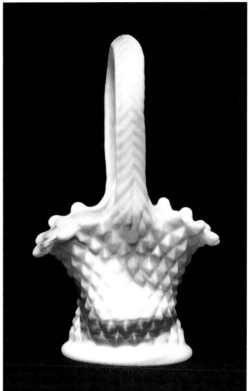

/475 Basket, 5 1/2",
Ruby Slag. $35-40.

/661 Vase, 5", Jade Slag. $60-65.

/860 Footed Bowl and Cover, 9 1/2",
Caramel Slag. $75-80.

/74C 3-Toed Bowl, 8", Rose, Jade Slag. $50-55.

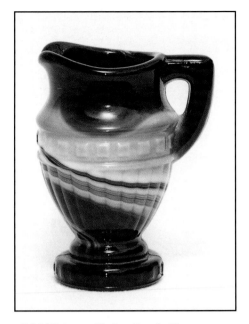

/104 Miniature Pitcher, Purple Slag. $30-35.

/720 Bell, Purple Slag. $55-60.

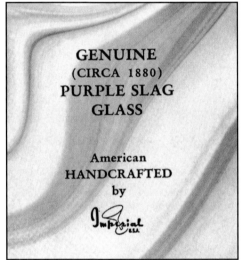

/1776 Federal Footed Cigarette Holder, Ruby Slag. $40-45.

"Genuine (Circa 1880) Purple Slag Glass" POPA Tag. Imperial Purple Slag was produced from 1959 to 1975. The date on the front of this tag simply relates to the method they were using. As related on the inside of this tag, "Challinor, Taylor and Company of Tarentum, Pennsylvania, was the leading EARLY 19th Century producer of Quality Purple Slag Glass. They secured their original methods and glass-mixes through English Inheritance and this good fortune was indeed valuable because England in the early 1800s made the FINEST and TRUEST Purple Slag in all the world! Challinor and Taylor, however, SOON captured the American Market. Imperial produces as closely as possible to the original English and Challinor-Taylor methods and standards."

/146, 4 1/2" Duck-on-Nest, Caramel Slag and Purple Slag. $50-55 each.

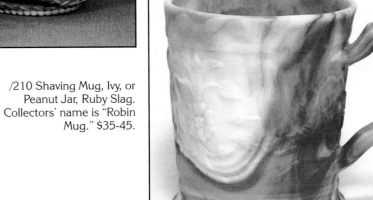

/210 Shaving Mug, Ivy, or Peanut Jar, Ruby Slag. Collectors' name is "Robin Mug." $35-45.

/156 Box and Cover or Marmalade Jar, Caramel Slag. $35-45.

/294, 4 1/2" Heart Ash Tray, Ruby Slag. If you look closely you might see the raised design of bow and arrows. They are difficult to see in a slag item. $25-30.

/965, 10" Footed Vase, Ruby Slag. $85-95.

/1591 Storybook Mug, Ruby Slag. $45-50.

End O' Day Ash Trays 1608/1—1962

End O' Day ash trays were made in 1962 in Green/White, Caramel/White, and Dark Blue/White. This is the only time that the Blue/White slag combination is shown. Note that this group of End O' Day ash trays predates all slag except purple slag.

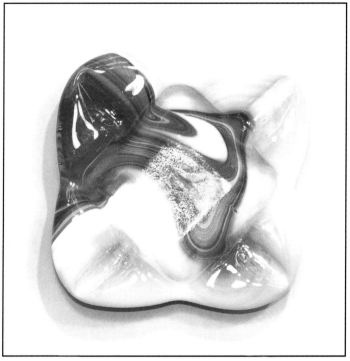

/1608/1 End O' Day Ash Tray, 7", Blue Slag. Blue slag is seldom found. $30-40.

/1608/1 End O'Day Ash Tray, 7", Caramel Slag. $30-40.

Caramel Slag Animals—1969-1977

From 1969 to 1977 Imperial produced animals in Caramel Slag. Those marked with an asterisk were from Imperial molds, those marked with H were from Heisey molds, and those marked with C were from Cambridge molds. None were made in satin finish.

Mold	Company	Lenox Name	Lenox No.
1	H	Donkey	43941
2	H	Elephant	43942
5/1	*	Pup	43943
5/2	*	Pup	
5/3	*	Pup	
5/4	*	Pup	43944
8	H	Sittin' Duck	43938
9/1	H	Mallard (Wings Straight-Up)	43939
9/2	H	Mallard (Wings Half-Up)	43940
9/3	H	Mallard (Wings Down)	
11	H	Scotty Champ	
12/1	H	Pony Stallion	43945
12/2	H	"Balking" Colt	
12/3	H	"Standing" Colt	43946
12/4	H	"Kicking" Colt	
14	H	Champ Terrier	43947
18	*	Hoot (Less) Owl	43948
19	*	Woodchuck	43949
	H	Elephant	43933
	H	Bunny	43935
	H	Cygnet	43936
	C	Scottie Bookend	43951

Caramel Slag—1982

Below are the twenty-six Caramel Slag items produced by Imperial in 1982.

Lenox Number	Description
43154	36 oz. Pitcher
43199	6 1/4" Dog Candy Box and Cover
43401	10 3/4" Plate, Windmill
43487	Salt and Pepper
43528	3" Cornucopia
43530	Sugar and Cream
43580	8" Shell Ash Tray
43620	2 1/2" Toothpick
43641	7" Basket With Milk Glass Handle
43695	8 1/2" Crimped Bowl, Windmill
43696	10" Crimped Bowl, Grape
43721	5" Footed Compote
43735	9 1/2" Footed Compote and Cover
43738	6 1/2" Footed Crimp Compote
43759	6" Vase
43763	6 1/4" Footed Vase
43771	9 1/2" Footed Vase
43835	4 1/2" Minuet Girl
43863	5" Dog Collar Ash Tray
43890	5" Pie Wagon and Cover
43931	Scolding Bird
43933	Elephant
43935	Bunny
43936	Cygnet
43951	Scottie Book End
43957	Tiger Paper Weight

Milk Glass With Colored Glass

Provincial—1962-1966

In 1962, Imperial had a line of Provincial Stems and a 7 1/2" plate. This line has a prefix of 56/. The goblet, sherbet, juice, and footed ice tea came in either Milk Glass or Turquoise Opaque. Other common colors were Amber, Azalea, and Verde, which were done in 1966.

56/   12 oz. Goblet
56/   8 oz. Sherbet
56/   7 oz. Footed Juice or Wine
56/   16 oz. Footed Ice Tea
56/   7 1/2" Plate (made to go with the Provincial but
       in milk glass only)

/56 Provincial Cordial in Turquoise Opaque. The cordial is not on the company production list we have, yet we do know of several of these cordials. In 1989, four cordials in Turquoise and Milk Glass were bought at the Hay Shed, a Bellaire, Ohio, glass consignment shop. $15-20.

"CONTINENTAL"
95/176 Royal Cobalt

"PROVINCIAL"
56 Forest

| 12 oz. Goblet | 7 oz. Sherbet | 2 oz. Cordial | 4½ oz. Cocktail | 6 oz. Wine | 12 oz. Ftd. Iced Tea | 12 oz. Goblet | 8 oz. Sherbet | 4 oz. Cocktail | 7 oz. Ftd. Juice or Wine | 16 oz. Ftd. Iced Tea |

"PROVINCIAL"
56

Larkspur Blue　　　　　　*Milk Glass*

| 12 oz. Goblet | 8 oz. Sherbet | 4 oz. Cocktail | 7 oz. Ftd. Juice or Wine | 16 oz. Ftd. Iced Tea | 12 oz. Goblet | 8 oz. Sherbet | 7 oz. Ftd. Juice or Wine | 16 oz. Ftd. Iced Tea |

"PROVINCIAL"
56

Turquoise Opaque　　　　　　*Topaz*

| 12 oz. Goblet | 8 oz. Sherbet | 7 oz. Ftd. Juice or Wine | 16 oz. Ftd. Iced Tea | 12 oz. Goblet | 8 oz. Sherbet | 4 oz. Cocktail | 7 oz. Ftd. Juice or Wine | 16 oz. Ftd. Iced Tea |

HAND PAINTED WESTERN APPLE

| 176/Dec. 12 oz. Goblet | 176/Dec. 7 oz. Sherbet | 176/Dec. 6 oz. Wine | 176/Dec. Footed Finger Bowl or Dessert | 176/Dec. 12 oz. Footed Iced Tea | 176/Dec. 80 oz. Pitcher |

(See Price List For Other Items Available in Western Apple)

IMPERIAL GLASS CORPORATION, BELLAIRE, OHIO

Imperial supplemental catalog page from 1962 showing the /56 Provincial stems in both Milk Glass and Turquoise Opaque. $10-15 each.

Parisian Provincial—1962

The 1962 Supplement One Catalog included a #563 Parisian Provincial line, consisting of the same stems as the Provincial line. These items had milk glass stems with bowls of Amber, Heather, Verde, or Ruby. The line also included a 7 1/2" Plate in milk glass and a 4 3/4" Nappy in the same color as the bowl on the stems.

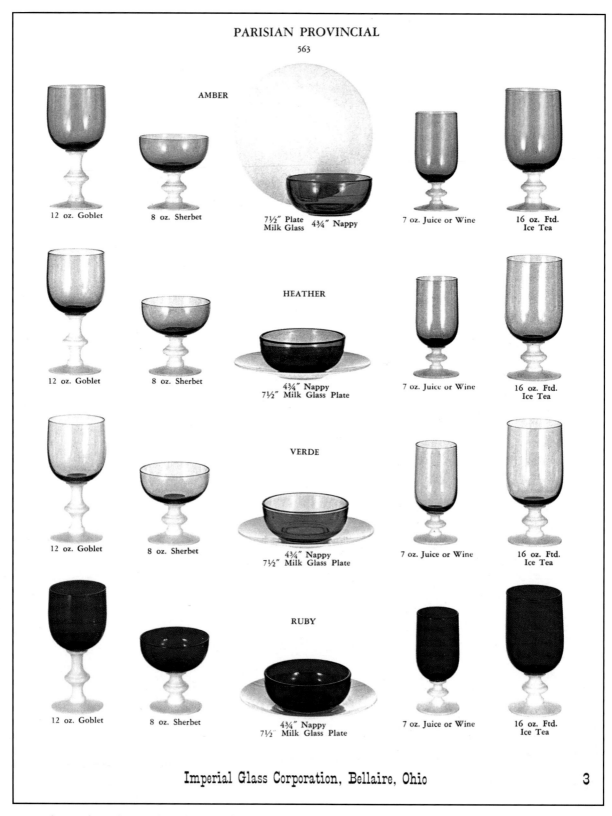

Imperial supplemental catalog page from 1962 showing the #563 Parisian Provincial stems. $15-20 each.

Hobnail Footed Bowl and Cover—1962

This Hobnail Footed Bowl and Cover, which is a scarce item, was also shown in the 1962 Supplement One Catalog. The cover and the stem of the bowl are milk glass and the bowl is either Heather, Amber, Mustard, or Antique Blue.

#615 Hobnail Footed Bowl and Cover, 7 1/2", Amber. Other available colors were Heather, Mustard, and Antique Blue. $40-45.

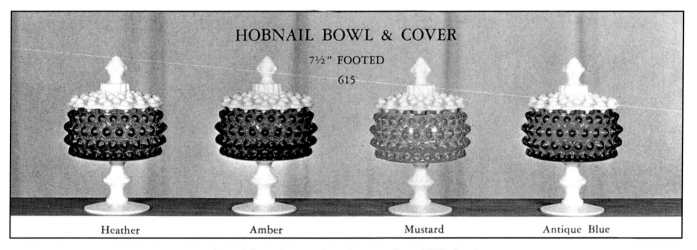

Imperial supplemental catalog page from 1962 showing the Hobnail Bowl and Cover in all four colors.

Peach Blow Decanter, Velvet Finished (Doeskin). Cased glass with ruby over the interior milk glass. During the making of Peach Blow, the heating process causes it to change to yellow and ruby. $200-250.

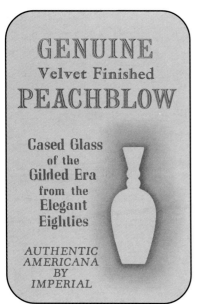

GENUINE
Velvet Finished
PEACHBLOW

Cased Glass
of the
Gilded Era
from the
Elegant
Eighties

AUTHENTIC
AMERICANA
BY
IMPERIAL

"Genuine Velvet Finished Peachblow" POPA tag. The inside of the tag provides background on this type of treatment:

"Of the late 19th century glass "Fancy Wares" none exemplified greater artistry, beauty and skill than Peachblow. Genuine 'originals' are extremely rare today! In 1886 William Leighton, Jr., of Hobbs, Brockunier & Company, (operating a factory started in 1845) made the first *Wheeling Peachblow* and the item was a Vase copied from a famed one-of-its-kind Chinese Porcelain called Peachblow, known as the 'Morgan Vase' and named after its then owner Mary J. Morgan. This Porcelain brought $18,000 at public auction back in 1886 at New York City. Quite a price! It was only 8" tall and is profiled on the face of this Story-Brochure."

"Leighton's Peachblow Glass Vase was an exact copy of the Morgan Porcelain, both in shape AND color. One of these 1886 Hobbs, Brockunier *Originals* is in the J. Ralph Boyd Memorial Glass Collection of the Mansion Museum, Oglebay Park, Wheeling, West Virginia, where it is on public exhibit. It was made by gathering 'Gold Ruby' Glass over a Milk Glass 'gob' and this procedure was and still is called 'casing,' or 'plating.' The Pipe-blown Vase was then carefully heat-struck in a fiery Glory Hole to get the genuine *Wheeling Peachblow* characteristic—exquisite color-shading from deepest Ruby to a delicate yellow-green."

"The Handcrafted Skills necessary to accomplish the Imperial Reproductions of '*Wheeling Peachblow*' are based on long, tedious research and trials. They attest to Imperial's proud position as The House of Americana Glassware. Basically our Peachblow methods are those of 1886. Raw Materials today are unlike those of a hundred years ago. Melting Vessels and fuels are different and skills are not the same, so these genuine Peachblow vases are proud achievements! Gifts from Imperial always have Heritage, each one a 'story' and they weave simplicity, antiquity and uniquity into lovely, decorative and useful articles for Gracious Living."

#001 Banjo and #002 Fiddle. These vases are made by the workman gathering milk glass and then dropping the gathering rod into the desired color; amber and verde green in these examples. This is referred to as cased glass. $40-50 each.

POPA tag for the Banjo & Fiddle Vases. This eye-catching tag identifies these vases as "Genuinely American Pipe Blown by Imperial—USA."

This label referring to "Genuine American Cased Glass" was placed on the #001 Banjo and #002 Fiddle by Imperial. $40-50 each.

White Ice—1977

White Ice was a new line introduced in 1977. Imperial described it as "Opaque beauty and grace. Eleven satin-finished Milk Glass shapes, handblown and finished by master craftsmen. Thoroughly contemporary in design. As pleasing to the eye as a work of art."[17]

The items are exactly as named in the 1977 catalog, and they have no design on the surface. The following numbers are those used in the Lenox era.

Lenox Number	Description
51673	7" Noorvik Vase
51682	3 1/2" Barrow Bowl, Narrow
51684	5 1/2" Barrow Bowl
51688	3 1/2" Barrow Bowl, Wide
51754	4 1/2" Nome Vase
51764	8" Kodiak Vase
51766	8" Sitka Vase
51768	9" Noorvik Vase
51770	10" Sitka Vase
51772	10" Kodiak Vase
51776	12" Kodiak Vase

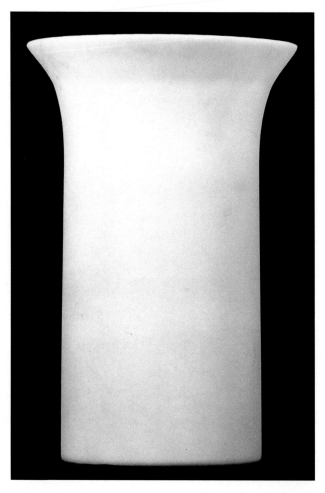

White Ice 10" Kodiak Vase, #51772. This is one of eleven pieces made in White Ice. $45-50.

Milk Glass Heisey Animals—1977-1978, 1988

Imperial made limited edition Milk Glass animals from Heisey molds for the Heisey Collectors of America. All are marked with the IG. According to Imperial documentation, the following animals were made:

Rabbit Paperweight	1977
Heads Up Bunny	1977
Heads Down Bunny	1977
Mother Rabbit	1978
Hen	1978
Chick Head Up	1978
Chick Head Down	1978
Rooster	1978
Scotty	1978
Pony Stallion	1978

Imperial made small quantities of a few other milk glass animals from Heisey molds, probably during the same time period as those above. We have seen these animals: Sittin' Duck, Standing Colt, Plug Horse, Mallard Wings Up, Mallard Wings Half Up, Donkey, and Elephant.

The Heisey Mother Rabbit weighs 3 1/4 pounds—that is a lot of milk glass! Note the IG mark on the rabbit's front leg.

Heisey Animals made by Imperial. From left: Mother Rabbit, Heads Up Bunny, Heads Down Bunny, Rabbit Paperweight, Scottie, Chick Head Down, Chick Head Up, Rooster, Hen. Mother Rabbit $65-70. Others $10-40 each according to size.

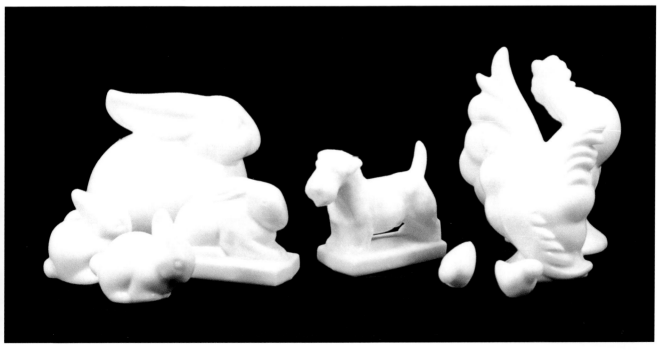

Swung Vases

Pictured below is an undated Imperial promotion photograph for swung vases. From the early days of Imperial, the company used the idea of swinging a pressed or blown item while the glass was still hot and pliable, thus creating a different item. The milk glass examples in our collection do have the IG mark on the bottom, so that places this promotion after 1951.

We have found similar examples of Cape Cod and Candlewick pieces being "swung" to make a whimsy. These items were never in the regular line and were most likely done by workmen on a "whim."

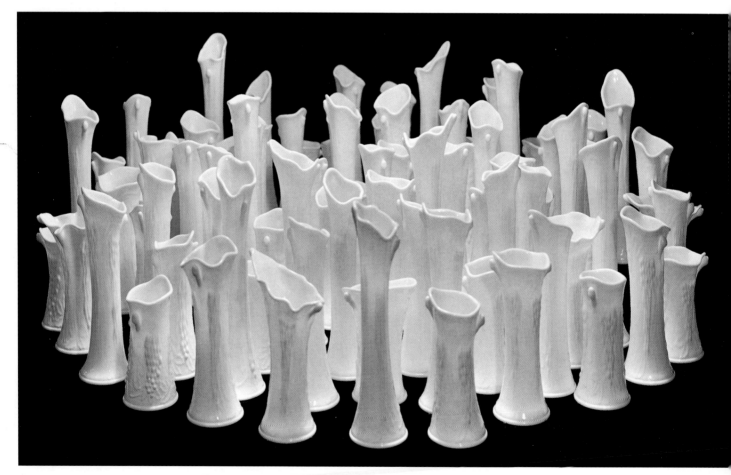

This Imperial promotional photo shows swung vases made from a 1950/893 Jar. While hot and still attached to the worker's punty rod, the pieces were swung to achieve the desired effect. $25-40 each.

Private Mold Customers

Imperial Glass Corporation produced glassware for many different distributors and private mold customers in addition to the glass that it produced for its own general line. "Private mold" work meant that Imperial would either use the customers' own molds to make glass for them or Imperial would create the molds for glassware to be made for a special customer. Additionally, Imperial used its own general line molds to make special orders for customers. Shown here is a selection of private mold customers and the milk glass items purchased from Imperial.

Irving W. Rice

There were many customers who fit the private mold category, however the company we have researched the most is the Irving W. Rice Company, often called Irice.

Irice was a distributor of dresser accessories, salt and peppers, and other related items. From the early 1940s to the 1950s, Imperial supplied countless perfumes, colognes, puff boxes, mirrors, and so on to Irice.

While doing research for our book *Imperial's Boudoir, Etcetera*, we were puzzled by the name "Dolly Madison," a decoration on a milk glass dresser set made by Imperial for Irving W. Rice. Then we remembered an Imperial catalog page showing the "Dolly Madison" decoration on a sugar and cream and hastened to make a comparison with the dresser set we had found. They were one and the same! Now we could connect an Irice set with the Imperial hand decoration. Knowing one line or group of Imperial Glass will often answer questions in other lines and this is a good example. The same is true for items made in milk glass. Many, many of them were made in other colors during different years of Imperial's

E-750WN, 5" Cologne, and E-750J, 3 1/4" Square Box, made for Irving W. Rice, 1942-1945. Most collectors would not guess that this is an Imperial product. $225-275 set.

production. Knowing what colors an item was made in helps collectors spot a reproduction that may happen into the market after Imperial was out of business.

As noted, Imperial included many dresser sets and related items in their long production life. The Hobnail and Scroll patterns included cologne bottles and puff boxes. There were also puff boxes and boudoir boxes that did not belong to a specific pattern line. Through extensive research of Imperial's relationship with Irving W. Rice, we have documented several more milk glass dresser sets. Imperial's large production of dresser items for Irving W. Rice in the 1940s is thoroughly discussed in our book *Imperial's Boudoir, Etcetera . . .A Comprehensive Look at Dresser Accessories for Irice and Others*, © 1996. Below are photos of milk glass dresser sets made by Imperial for Irving W. Rice.

E-750NN and E-750WN. Here is a classic example of colognes coming with a narrow neck and a wide neck. It took several years to find these two bottles and finally to understand the meaning of the factory papers and identification numbers with NN and WN— Narrow Neck and Wide Neck. $95-120 each.

E-557 Dresser Set, Opal, gold strips, made for Irving W. Rice, 1942-1944. $120-130 set.

E-510 Dresser Set with Dolly Madison hand-painted decoration, made for Irving W. Rice, 1942-1946. $115-125 set.

Metropolitan Museum of Art and Smithsonian Institution

Imperial distinguished itself by being chosen to reproduce items for the Metropolitan Museum of Art. These items carried the Metropolitan Museum of Art's hallmark (MMA) to identify them as reproductions and were made to be sold in the museum's gift shops. The Cache Pot was made from 1976 to 1980. From 1979 to 1982, the Flower Pot and Saucer was produced. The MMA would not allow its special pieces to leave the museum, as they were virtually irreplaceable. Instead, the museum made a plaster cast of the pieces to be copied and Imperial made the mold from this plaster cast. In the 1970s and 1980s, Imperial was given permission to produce several items in color to be sold through its own channels.

Metropolitan Museum of Art, Flower Pot and Saucer. $40-45.

Metropolitan Museum of Art, Flower Pot and Saucer in Opaque Blue. $45-50.

Metropolitan Museum of Art Certificate of Authenticity. This enclosure was placed in the box with every Flower Pot and Stand to identify it as an authorized copy of the original.

In the 1970s, the Smithsonian Institution also relied on Imperial to produce items for its museum. Those special items to be reproduced were brought to the factory, and then the mold was made. An SI mark was placed in the molds made for the Smithsonian Institution. Some of the pieces copied were from the old pattern glass known as Broken Column. The Smithsonian gift shop

items were made in crystal. In later years (c. 1980-1982) Imperial was able to sell several Smithsonian items marked with the SI in Imperial's own gift shop. We do not have any paper showing that Imperial made milk glass items for the Smithsonian Institution.

Hotel and Restaurant Trade

Imperial sold glass through more outlets than just the usual department stores and gift stores. We have a 1963-1964 folder showing photos and price lists of items that Imperial supplied to the hotel and restaurant trade. In addition to the specific items listed, Imperial offered to do special orders with the crest of the specific business if desired. Special orders of any of Imperial's molds in a particular color were also possible, when ordered in large enough quantities. Offered in this folder were the following milk glass items:

1950/473	Vintage Grape 10 oz. Goblet
1950/216	Footed Salt and Pepper, Grape
1950/247	Salt and Pepper, Grape
1950/96	Salt and Pepper, Grape
1950/42	Salt and Pepper
1950/428	Basket
1950/4283	3 Piece Salt/Pepper/Tray 1950/42 and 1950/428
1950/291	4 1/2" Ash Tray, Atlantis
1950/293	4 1/2" Ash Tray, Grape
1950/520	9 1/2" Zodiac Ash Tray
1950/532	7" Ash Tray

F.W. Woolworth Company

In a letter dated 1951, an Imperial representative reported the sale of fifteen milk glass items in large quantities to the F.W. Woolworth Company. These items were from the general line that year. We found no other records of sales to this company, though one must remember that during the Imperial liquidation records became scattered and many papers were not saved.

Undocumented Items

It is likely that undocumented items will continue to appear on the scene. Their story may never be complete because the glass companies were always trying items for feasibility or for a special purpose. While researching our Cape Cod book, we were told that if a customer came to the factory and asked for a certain item to be made in a special color or decoration, it would be done if possible. Those pieces most likely never made the documentation trail. Workers often used unusual treatments on pieces they were working on and then took them home. Since the closing of the factory, these items are beginning to appear for sale as the former workers begin disposing of excess collections.

Imperial Candlewick collectors are interested in any undocumented information pertaining to Candlewick. For example, we have a 400/249, 5 1/2" Peg Nappy in milk glass. We have documentation for this item in crystal but not in milk glass. The peg nappy was found at the factory and bought during the liquidation of Imperial Glass Corporation. Another interesting item is the 400/109 Individual Salt and Pepper Set. This set was acquired at one of the National Imperial Glass Collectors' Society conventions. We have also seen the 400/74SC 9" Crimped Bowl in milk glass. It was made by one of the Imperial workers and then given to his neighbor who was an avid Candlewick collector. She shared with us the excitement of having this piece.

400/249 Candlewick Peg Nappy in Milk Glass. Undocumented item. $*

400/109 Candlewick Individual Salt and Pepper. Undocumented item. $*

On the cover of a 1968 Pillsbury cookbook is a 400/67D Low Cake Stand in milk glass. We have also seen the 400/2701 Two-Tier Tidbit used in a food advertisement. We assume that Imperial may have made special pieces for this type of promotional use. We do know that Imperial supplied glassware to be used on Hollywood movie sets. The company also had many advertisements in leading magazines and from time to time these same publications would feature food displayed in some of Imperial's popular patterns.

Sixteen gorgeous servings of this six-layer beauty. Flaky butter pastry rounds alternated with vanilla pudding and luscious raspberry filling. Prepare everything early, then assemble 2 hours before serving.

Raspberry Ribbon Torte

Pastry
　2 cups Pillsbury's Best All Purpose Flour*
　¼ teaspoon salt
　1 cup butter or margarine, softened
　4 to 6 tablespoons water
　Sugar

Vanilla Filling
　1 package (3¾ oz.) instant vanilla
　　pudding mix
　1½ cups milk

Raspberry Filling
　2 tablespoons cornstarch
　¼ cup water
　1 package (10 oz.) frozen raspberries,
　　thawed and undrained

Topping
　1 cup whipping cream
　⅓ cup sugar
　¼ teaspoon almond extract

OVEN 450°　　　　　　　　16 SERVINGS

Pastry: In large mixing bowl, combine flour and salt. Cut in butter until particles are the size of small peas. Add water, a little at a time, tossing and stirring lightly with fork. Form into a ball; divide into six equal por-

tions. Roll out each portion on floured surface to a 9-inch circle; cut around an inverted 9-inch pie pan to even edges. Transfer each circle to a cool baking sheet. Prick generously with fork; sprinkle each with about 1½ teaspoons sugar. Bake at 450° for 5 to 7 minutes, until golden brown. Remove from cookie sheet. Cool thoroughly. Within 2 hours of serving time, stack layers, spreading Vanilla and Raspberry Fillings alternately between layers, ending with Raspberry layer on top. Spread Topping on sides and around top edge of Torte. Serve within 2 hours.

Vanilla Filling: In small mixing bowl, combine instant pudding mix and milk. Prepare as directed on package. Chill thoroughly.

Raspberry Filling: In small saucepan, combine cornstarch and water; add raspberries with syrup. Cook over medium heat, stirring constantly, until thick. Cool.

Topping: In small mixing bowl, combine Topping ingredients. Beat until thickened.

*For use with Pillsbury's Best Self-Rising Flour, omit salt in Pastry.

129

Page 129 of Pillsbury's Bake Off Dessert Cook Book also shows the undocumented 400/67D Low Cake Stand in milk glass. It was used to illustrate this tempting dessert. *Image shown here with permission of the Pillsbury Company.*

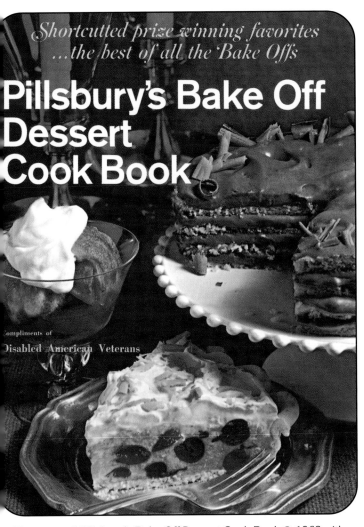

The cover of *Pillsbury's Bake Off Dessert Cook Book* © 1968 with a second printing in 1971. Note the Imperial Candlewick (400/67D) Low Cake Stand in milk glass that any avid Candlewick collector would love to have! *Cover shown here with permission of the Pillsbury Company.* $*

We know of eleven pieces of Imperial's 400/Candlewick line that have been found in Caramel Slag, though production dates for these items have not been documented. We do know that when most of these items were made in crystal they have a common production date of 1965, which is also the date that Caramel Slag first appeared in catalogs. One of the Candlewick items (400/174) was only produced in crystal until 1963, but that does not preclude the use of that mold for a piece made in Caramel Slag. We therefore think that 1965 can safely be assumed as the production date for the

Caramel Slag items as well. Perhaps the 400/174 item that was made in crystal until 1963 was the first (and perhaps) experimental piece of Candlewick made in slag. Below are the Candlewick items that we have seen in the Caramel Slag.

400/42D	5 3/4" Plate
400/52B	6 1/2" Bowl 2 Handled
400/52D	7 1/2" Plate 2 Handled
400/62D	8 1/2" Plate
400/145C	12" Plate Crimped
400/145D	12" Plate 2 Handle
400/150	6" Ash Tray
400/174	6 1/2" Heart
400/182	8 1/2" Bowl 3-Toed
400/183	6" Bowl 3-Toed
400/256	10 1/2" Relish Oval Divided

We have seen items in the Tradition #165 line from the 1930s in milk glass. Our collection includes a 6" Vase #330 (AKA "Diamond Block"), from the same time period. The #330 is covered with raised diamond shapes and has a raised dot at each diamond point. There are also a few milk glass items made in the Chroma #123 line. In the 1930s, the #699 line was called Mt. Vernon. A.H. Heisey & Company had already been using this name for several years, so Imperial changed their Mt. Vernon name to Washington #699. The Washington pattern has a pattern of cubes similar to the Fostoria American pattern and several items have been found in milk glass. Since our information is so sparse for this period, undoubtedly more milk glass was produced that we will learn about as time goes on.

400/256 Relish, Caramel Slag. $300-325.

Tradition #165. This pattern may be found in limited numbers in milk glass. $20-25.

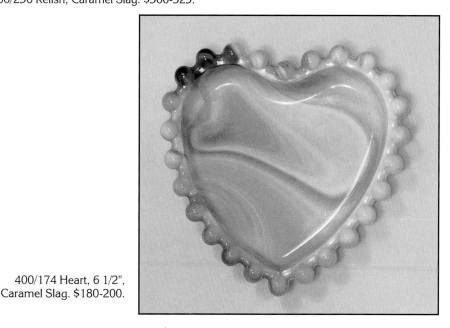

400/174 Heart, 6 1/2", Caramel Slag. $180-200.

Washington #699. For identification only. This pattern may be found in limited numbers in milk glass.

"Diamond Block" #330. This pattern may also be found in limited numbers in milk glass. $25-30.

Chroma #123. For identification only. This pattern may be found in limited numbers in milk glass.

These next photographs are included to show you some additional unknown items. We do not have a clue to the story of this Ski Tumbler, but we want collectors to be aware of it. Although marked with the IG on the bottom, it does not have any of the characteristics of other Imperial milk glass. The glass is thinner and the design is raised on the outside and recessed on the inside. It appears to be hand-painted over an iridescent surface. Several tumblers, both painted and unpainted, were found in North Carolina.

Two views of the Ski Tumbler are shown to give a complete picture. This undocumented tumbler is marked with the IG mark yet is an entirely different quality from the general milk glass. It is much thinner and seems to have an iridescent finish. We were told the tumblers were both decorated and undecorated. There is no company documentation on this item. $*

The milk glass for this 9 oz. /489 Rose Tumbler is like the items made in the 1930s-1940s. It has a "skim milk" look rather than the "whole milk" white color of the 1950s. The /489 Tumbler and 400/24 Pitcher were shown only in the 1950 catalog. We are uncertain if this hand-painted decoration was applied for the general public or if it was an employee's item. We do know of four of the tumblers, and they came from the factory area. We do not think it fits the "Polychrome" treatment. We are including it here so that collectors will know that it is Imperial glass.

Imperial made large amounts of glass parts for several lighting companies. Some have been documented in our book *Imperial's Boudoir, Etcetera . . . A Comprehensive Look at Dresser Accessories for Irice and Others*. In the future, examples of this market will continue to surface and hopefully, so will more documentation. One table lamp with an Imperial bowl has been found and added to an Imperial collection. The pieces of the puzzle are sure to gradually fit together.

1950/489 Rose Tumbler. Shown here so collectors will be aware of its existence. We have found no information on this tumbler. It is not the "Polychrome Decoration." $*

Table Lamp made from the 1950/47 Grape Bowl. Imperial sold many glass parts to private light fixture companies. So far we have found no paper documentation for the sale of milk glass parts, but here is an example showing that such milk glass parts were sold to light fixture companies. $*

Part III
Imperial Patterns and Categories

Patterns—Photographs and Catalog Illustrations

"Candlewick"

1950/75C, 11" Crimped Fruit Bowl, "Candlewick." $60-65.

1950/196, 2 Piece Epergne Set, "Candlewick." $80-100.

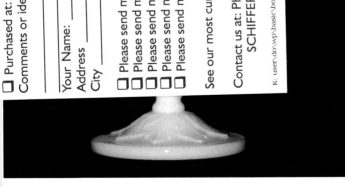

1950/75H, 9" Heart Fruit or Dessert, "Candlewick." $100-125.

Catalog Illustrations

1950/75C	11" Crimped Fruit Bowl, "Candlewick"
	1950-52 $60-65
1950/75D	11" Buffet or Wall Plate, "Candlewick"
	1950-52 $60-65
1950/75F	11" Coupe Apple Bowl, "Candlewick"
	1950-51 $60-65
1950/103	10" Footed Fruit Bowl, "Candlewick"
	1950-60 $60-70

1950/75C 11"
Crimped Fruit Bowl

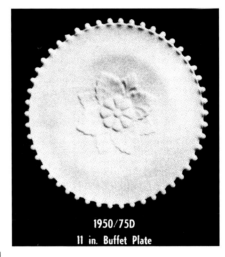

1950/75D
11 in. Buffet Plate

1950/75F 11"
Couped Apple Bowl

1950/103
10" Footed Fruit Bowl

1950/45, 5" Jelly Comporte, "Candlewick." The style shown here does not have the vertical lines below the beads on the outside, nor does it have a flower design on the interior. The later style does have the vertical lines and the flower design. $35-40.

1950/196	2 Piece Epergne, "Candlewick"	1950-60	$80-100
1950/750	3 Piece Heart Tid Bit Or Ash Tray, "Candlewick"	1950-64	$45-50
1950/170	Low Candleholder, "Candlewick"	1950-60	$20-25

| 1950/45 | 5" Jelly Comporte, "Candlewick" | 1950-60 | $35-40 |
| 1950/75H | 9" Heart Fruit or Dessert, "Candlewick" | 1950-52 | $100-125 |

1950/196
10" 2-pc. Epergne Set

1950/45
5" Jelly Comporte

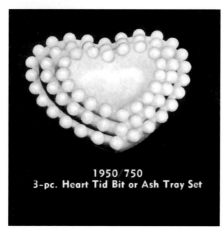

1950/750
3-pc. Heart Tid Bit or Ash Tray Set

1950/75H   9"
Heart Fruit or Dessert Bowl

1950/170
Low Candleholder

A detail of interest to Candlewick collectors is the design of the 1950/103, 1950/196, and 1950/45 items. All were made with vertical exterior lines and raised leaf design on the interior. These same pieces were also made without the exterior lines and the interior raised leaf design.

Additional Candlewick items may be seen in the chapter showing Undocumented Items, which begins on page 70. These items include an undocumented 400/67D Cake Plate in milk glass (shown on the cover of *Pillsbury's Bake Off Dessert Cook Book* from 1968) and an undocumented 400/109 Salt and Pepper Set in milk glass. The 400/249 mold was used to make an undocumented peg nappy. It, too, is shown in the undocumented chapter.

Cape Cod

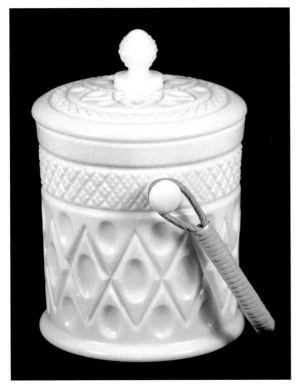

1950/200, 5" Mug or Ivy Holder, Cape Cod. $60-65.

1950/94, 4 1/2" x 5" Candy Jar and Cover, with Handle, Cape Cod. $65-75.

1950/1602 Cigarette Lighter, Cape Cod. Cape Cod lighters are available in the five colors shown here: Nut Brown, Ruby, Black, Milk Glass, and Purple Slag. $35-45 each.

Catalog Illustrations

1950/94	4 1/2" x 5" Candy Jar and Cover with Handle, Cape Cod	1952-55	$65-75
1950/193	3 1/2" x 4" Jar and Cover with Handle, Cape Cod	1952-53	$85-95
1950/200	5" Mug or Ivy Holder, Cape Cod	1950-55	$60-65
1950/1602	Cigarette Lighter, Cape Cod	1962-66	$40-45

1950/94
4½" x 5" Candy Jar & Cover,
with Handle

1950 193
3½" x 4"
Jar & Cover with Handle

Milk Glass

1950/1602
Cigarette Lighter

1950/200
5" Mug Ivy Holder

Grape

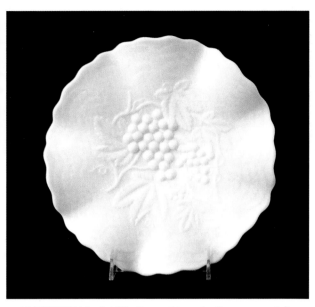

1950/47, 8" Berry Bowl, Grape. $20-22.

11/4736C Dish, 9 1/2", Grape. Note the lines around the outer perimeter, a feature characteristic of the older pieces. The dish is also decorated with grapes on the underside. $20-25.

1950/473, 9 oz. Tumbler, Grape. $8-10.

1950/727C, 4" Footed, Crimped Bowl, Grape. $15-17.

1950/842, 4 1/2" Nappy, 2 Handles and 1950/851, 5" Nappy Handled, Grape. $8-10 each.

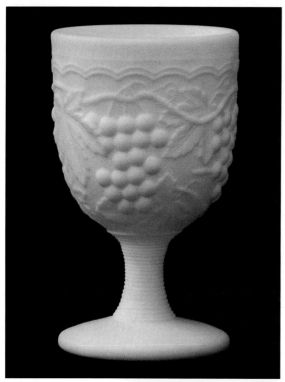

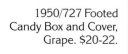

1950/473, 10 oz.
Goblet, Grape. $8-18.

1950/900 Covered Sugar and
Cream, Grape. $20-22 set.

1950/727 Footed
Candy Box and Cover,
Grape. $20-22.

1950/114, 7 1/4"
Lamp Vase,
Crimped, Grape.
$25-27.

1950/216 Footed Salt and Pepper, Grape.
$18-20 set.

1950/115, 10 3/4"
Footed Lamp Vase,
Crimped, Grape.
$40-45.

1950/21, 6" Vase, Grape. $15-17.

1950/216, 7 3/4" Boutique
Lamp, Grape. $50-55.

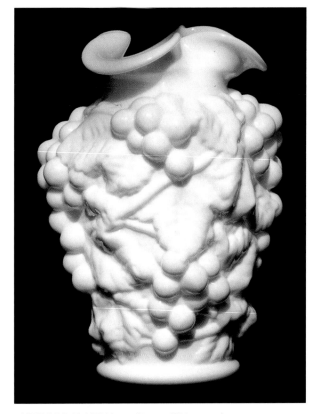

1950/180, 7 1/2" Vase, Grape. This vase has a very
different blown effect to the design. It is unknown if the
item was influenced by the early 1900s Goofus Glass.
$18-20.

11/473C, 6" Compote, Footed, Grape. $12-15.

1950/858, 6" Handled Pickle Tray, Grape. $20-22.

1950/893 Jar and Cover with Wicker Handle, Grape. $60-65.

1950/123 Toast Plate and Cover, Grape. Consists of 8" Cupped Plate and clear cover with hollow knob. The same cover is used on the Candlewick and Cape Cod Toast Plates. $95-110.

1950/128 15 Piece Punch Set, Grape. Note the black hangers for the cups; the set was sold with hangers from the factory. *Imperial Glass Photograph.* $175-185 for set.

A 1950/128 10 Piece Punch Set, Grape, is shown in the center of this photograph. The ladle in this set for 1950 was listed as Christmas Green, though we have never seen a Christmas Green ladle. (Note that the small vase, second from left in back row, was originally unknown. Unexpectedly, however, an undated catalog page was discovered showing this vase in crystal as #1186, 4" Blown Vase). *Imperial Glass Photograph.* Punch Set $150-200 without ladle. Christmas Green ladle, rare $*

1186 4" Blown Vase
(available in Crystal & Colors. See price list)

This is the Imperial catalog illustration documenting the small vase in the photo at left as 1950/1186.

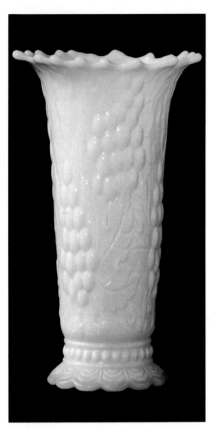

11/4732L, 7 1/2" Vase, Grape. This vase was made from the 11/4732B Vase. While still hot, it was swung to give it the stretched look. Imperial often created items using this method. $20-22.

1950/473, 3 Pint Pitcher, Grape, and 1950/473, 10 oz. Goblets. The Grape pattern is popular with collectors and this is an outstanding example of the detail in design that Imperial Glass Corporation produced. $98-163 set.

Catalog Illustrations

1950/1D	6 1/2" Plate, Grape	1954-68	$5-7
1950/3D	7 1/2" Plate, Grape	1954-69	$5-7
1950/5D	8 1/2" Plate, Grape	1954-66	$8-10
1950/6D	9 1/2" Plate, Grape	1954-71	$10-12
1950/375	10" Footed Cake Stand, Grape	1958-68	$40-45

1950/1D
6½" Plate

1950/3D
7 1/2" Plate

1950/5D
8 1/2" Plate

1950/6D
9 1/2" Plate

1950/375
10" Footed Cake Stand

1950/296	10 1/2" Tray, Grape	1951-52	$35-40	
1950/716	8" Wall Plate, Grape, (no picture)	1954-55	$*	
1950/717	10" Wall Plate, Grape (no picture)	1954-55	$*	
1950/4735	6" Plate, Grape	1952-55	$8-10	
1950/4736	8" Plate, Grape	1952-55	$10-12	
1950/4738	10" Plate, Grape	1951-55	$18-20	
11/4736	9 1/2" Dish (same number as 8 3/4" Dish)	1930s	$20-25	

11/4738D	12" Plate, Grape	1943-43	$25-30
11/4738D	12" Cake Plate on Stand, 2 Pieces, Grape	1943-43	$45-50
1950/6C	8" Crimped Bowl, Grape	1954-71	$10-12

1950/296   10½"
Tray, Candy or Nut Dish, Grape

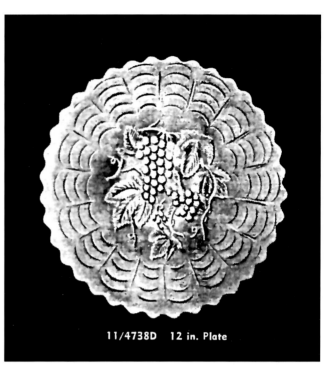

11/4738D   12 in. Plate

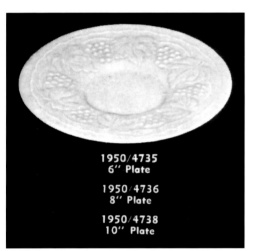

1950/4735
6" Plate

1950/4736
8" Plate

1950/4738
10" Plate

11/4736C   9½ in. Dish

11/4738D   12 in. Cake Plate,
on Stand, 2-pcs.

1950/6C
8" Crimped Bowl

1950/47	8" Berry Bowl, Grape	1952-71	$20-22
1950/47C	9" Crimped Bowl, Grape	1954-71	$20-22
1950/49	4 1/2" Berry Bowl, Grape (51552)	1952-67, 1978-78	$8-10
1950/32	5" Fruit, Grape (in 1950/8532 Set)	1952-60	$6-8
1950/468C	6 3/4" Bowl, Grape	1959-69	$12-15

1950/727C	4" Footed Crimp Bowl, Grape	1958-71	$15-17
1950/842	4 1/2" 2 Handled Nappy, Grape	1953-64	$8-10
1950/851	5" Handled Nappy, Grape (51570)	1953-59, 1978-78	$8-10
11/7003/4	4 1/2" Fruit Nappy, Grape (no picture)	1932	$10-12
11/7005/4	6 1/2" Nappy, Grape (no picture)	1932	$10-12
11/7007/4	9" Fruit Bowl, Grape (no picture)	1932	$15-20

1950 47
8" Berry Bowl

1950 468C
6¾" Bowl

1950/727C
4" Footed Crimped Bowl

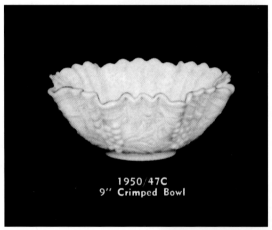

1950/47C
9" Crimped Bowl

1950 842
4½" 2-Handled Nappy

1950 49
4½" Berry Bowl

1950 851
5" Handled Nappy

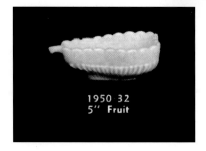

1950 32
5" Fruit

1950/859	11 1/2" Tall Footed Bowl and Cover, Grape	1956-60	$22-25
11/4738C	10 1/2" Crimped Fruit Bowl on Stand, Grape	1943	$70-75
11/4738N	8" Bulb Bowl, Grape	1943	$35-40
11/4738N	8" Bulb Bowl On Stand, Grape	1943	$70-75

1950/307	6 oz. Footed Tumbler, Grape	1955-62	$8-10
1950/473	9 oz. Tumbler, Grape (11/473)	1943, 1952-64	$8-10
1950/473	12 oz. Tumbler, Grape	1953-71	$8-10
1950/473	10 oz. Goblet, Grape (11/473)	1930,1943, 1951-71	$8-18
1950/473	6 oz. Sherbet, Grape	1951-68	$8-10
1950/473	3 oz. Wine, Grape (11/473)	1943, 1950-68	$10-12

1950/859
Bowl & Cover, 11½" Tall

1950/307
6 oz. Footed Tumbler

1950/473
9 oz. Tumbler

11/4738C 10½ in.
Crimped Fruit Bowl
on Stand

1950 473
12 oz. Tumbler

1950/473
10 oz. Goblet

11/4738N 8 in. Bulb Bowl

1950 473
6 oz. Sherbet

11/4738N 8 in. Bulb Bowl
on Stand

1950/473
3 oz. Wine

1950/4737	Cup and Saucer, Grape (11/473)	1943, 1951-69	$12-15
1950/4737	Punch Cup (same as above), Grape	1943, 1951-69	$7-8
1950/96	Salt and Pepper, Grape (51484)	1954-70, 1978-78	$15-20
1950/167	Duster or Shaker, Grape	1954-62	$15-20
1950/216	Footed Salt and Pepper, Grape	1956-71	$18-20
1950/247	Salt and Pepper, Grape	1951-71	$18-20

1950/682	Sugar and Cream Set 3-Toed, Grape	1952-71	$18-20
1950/831	Footed Sugar and Cream Set, Grape	1953-69	$20-22
1950/900	Covered Sugar and Cream Set, Grape (51535)	1955-68, 1978-78	$20-22
1950/901	Sugar and Cream Set, Grape	1955-69	$15-17

1950/4737
Cup and Saucer

1950/96
Salt & Pepper Set

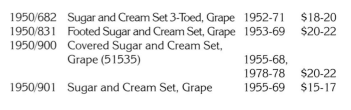

1950 682
Sugar and Cream Set (3-Toed)

1950/167
Duster-Shaker

1950/216
Footed Salt & Pepper

1950 831
Ftd. Sugar & Cream Set

1950 900
Covered Sugar and Cream Set

1950/247
Salt & Pepper Set

1950 901
Sugar and Cream Set

1950/468	4 1/4" Candy Jar and Cover, Grape (51880)	1958-68, 1978-78	$12-15
1950/727	Footed Candy Box and Cover, Grape	1955-71	$20-22
1950/735	Hex Candy Box and Cover, Grape	1956-71	$18-20
1950/810	Footed Candy Jar and Cover, Grape	1953-64	$18-20

1950/114	7 1/4" Lamp Vase Crimped, Grape	1955-60	$25-27
1950/115	10 3/4" Footed Lamp Vase Crimped, Grape	1956-60	$40-45
1950/179	8" Vase, Grape	1959-62	$25-30
1950/180	7 1/2" Vase, Grape	1955-68	$18-20
1950/191	Concord Ivy, Grape	1954-68	$18-20

1950 468
4¼" Candy Jar & Cover

1950/727
Ftd. Candy Box & Cover

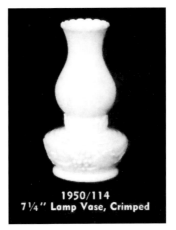

1950/114
7¼" Lamp Vase, Crimped

1950/115
10¾" Lamp Vase, Crimped

1950/735
Hex Candy Box & Cover

1950 179
8" Vase, Grape

1950/180
7½" Vase

1950 810
Ftd. Candy Jar & Cover

1950/191
Concord Ivy

1950/287	10" Vase, Grape (9" 11/4731C)	1943, 1953-65	$25-30
11/4732L	7 1/2" Vase, Grape	1930s	$20-22
1950/310	6" Bud Vase, Grape	1954-62	$12-15
1950/471/3	3 Section Ivy Tower, Grape	1958-68	$35-40
1950/472/4	4 Section Ivy Tower, Grape	1958-68	$45-50
1950/21	6" Vase, Grape	1930s,1943, 1950-69	$15-17
11/473	8" Blown Vase, Grape (no picture)	1932	$*
11/4732B	6" Vase	1932, 1943	$12-15
11/4732N	6" Vase, Grape	1930s	$20-22
11/4732K	6" Vase, Grape	1943	$20-22
11/473C	6" Compote	1932, 1943	$12-15
1950/128	15 Piece Punch Set, Grape (11/473)	1943, 1952-65	$175-185
1950/128	5 1/2" Punch Bowl Base, Grape	1943, 1952-65	$30-35
1950/128	Punch Bowl	1943, 1952-65	$40-45
	Christmas Green Ladle	1950-50	$70-75
1950/478	9 Piece Water Set, Grape (11/473)	1943, 1950-62	$110-120
1950/1630	9 Piece Wine Set, Grape (11/473)	1943, 1950-68	$135-140
1950/163	Decanter, Grape (11/473)	1943, 1950-68	$45-50

1950/21
6" Vase

11/4732B 6 in. Vase

11/4732N 6" Vase

11/4732K 6 in. Vase

11/473C 6 in. Compote

1950/287
10" Vase

11/4732L
7 1/2" Vase

1950/310
6" Bud Vase

1950 128
15-Pce. Punch Set, Crystal Ladle

1950 471
3 Section Ivy Tower

1950 472
4 Section Ivy Tower

1950/20	14 Piece Wassail Set, Grape	1950-50	$*
1950/8532	5 Piece Hors D'oeuvre Set	1951-60	$45-55
1950/420	14 Piece Tom and Jerry Set, Black Ladle	1953-55	$200-210

1950 478
9-Pce. Water Set
Consists of:
1—1950 473 3-Pint Pitcher with
8—1950 473 9 oz. Tumblers

1950/20
14 Pc. Wassail Set (Crystal Ladle)

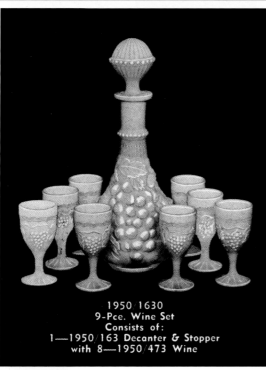

1950/1630
9-Pce. Wine Set
Consists of:
1—1950/163 Decanter & Stopper
with 8—1950/473 Wine

1950/8532
5-pc. Hors d'oeuvre Set

1950/163
Decanter & Stopper

1950/420
14 pc. Tom & Jerry Set
(5 quart)

1950/306	1 Quart Pitcher, Grape	1955-62	$40-45
1950/473	1 Pint Pitcher, Grape	1953-71	$30-35
1950/473	3 Pint Pitcher, Grape (11/473)	1943,	
		1951-69	$50-55

11/7003/4	6" Plate, Grape	1932	$10-12
11/7007/4	11" Service Plate, Grape,		
	(same as /7003/4)	1932	$15-20
11/7005/4	8" Salad Plate, Grape	1932	$10-12
11/473	10" Basket, Grape	1932, 1943	$40-45
1950/811	8 1/2" Oval Handled Basket,		
	Partitioned, Grape	1958-60	$45-50
1950/216	7 3/4" Boutique Lamp, Grape	1962-67	$50-55
1950/137	Double Candleholder, Grape	1959-61	$30-35
1950/880	3 1/2" Single Candleholder, Grape	1953-70	$10-12
1950/201	Cigarette Server, Grape	1950-69	$15-20

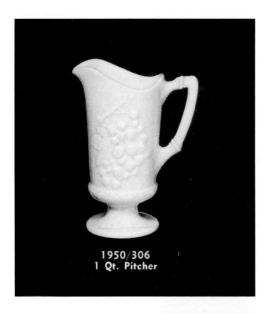

1950/306
1 Qt. Pitcher

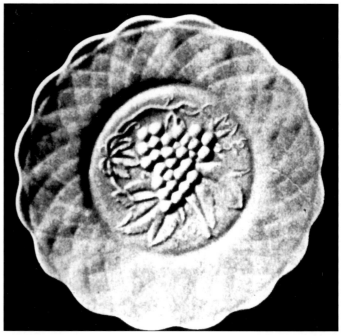

11/7003/4
6" Plate

11/7005/4
8" Plate

11/7007/4
11" Service Plate

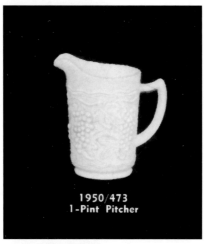

1950/473
1-Pint Pitcher

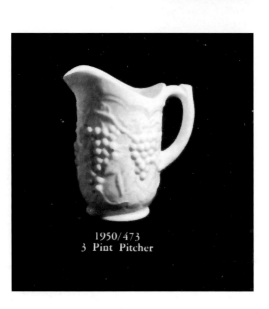

1950/473
3 Pint Pitcher

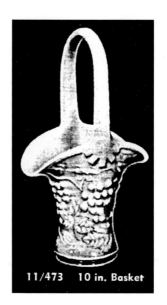

11/473   10 in. Basket

1950/811
8 ½" Oval Handled Basket, Partitioned

1950/3839
2-pc. Cigarette Set

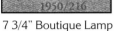

Milk Glass
1950/216
7 3/4" Boutique Lamp

1950 137
Double Candleholder

1950/225	Egg Cup, Grape	1954-62	$15-17
1950/241	Oil or Vinegar and Stopper, Grape	1953-65	$20-25
1950/433	Syrup Jar and Cover, Grape	1955-64	$18-20
1950/493	3 Piece Mayonnaise Set, Grape	1955-69	$22-25
1950/899C	2 Piece Sauce Set, Grape	1957-68	$15-17

1950/225
Egg Cup

1950/201
Cigarette Server

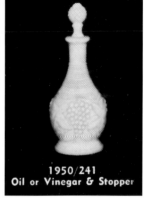

1950/241
Oil or Vinegar & Stopper

1950/433
Syrup Jar & Cover

1950 880
3 ½" Single Candleholder

1950/234	Handled Cigarette Box, Grape	1957-60	$15-20
1950/234/3	3 Piece Cigarette, Grape (no picture)	1957-60	$*
1950/293	4 1/2" Leaf Ash Tray, Grape (51850)	1951-69, 1977-78	$6-8
1950/38	6 oz. Pitcher (in /3839 Set), Grape	1954-64	$15-17
1950/39	Saucer (in /3839 Set)	1954-65	$8-10
1950/3839	2 Piece Cigarette Set, Grape	1954-64	$23-27

1950 493
3-Pce. Mayonnaise Set

1950/234
Handled Cigarette Box & Cover

1950 293
4 ¼" Grape Leaf Ash Tray

1950/899C
2-Pce. Sauce Set

1950/244	Handled Box and Cover, Grape	1957-65	$17-20
1950/244C	5" Handled Nappy Crimped, Grape	1959-69	$12-15
1950/255	7 1/2" 3 Partitioned Relish, Grape	1959-64	$40-45
1950/276	1/4 Pound Butter, Grape	1954-71	$30-35
1950/336	Box and Cover, Grape	1957-62	$18-20

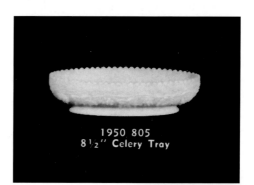

1950 805
8 1/2" Celery Tray

1950 244
Handled Box & Cover

1950 244C
5" Handled Nappy, Crimped

1950 858
6" Handled Pickle Tray

1950 255
7 1/2" 3 Partitioned Relish

1950 276
1/4 lb. Butter & Cover

1950 812
8 1/2" Relish, Partitioned

1950 336
Box & Cover

1950/893
Jar & Cover with Handle

1950/805	8 1/2" Celery, Grape	1953-66	$12-15
1950/858	6" Handled Pickle Tray, Grape	1953-66	$20-22
1950/812	8 1/2" Relish Partitioned, Grape	1958-62	$20-22
1950/893	Jar and Cover, With Wicker Handle, Grape	1953-60	$32-35
1950/899	Covered Marmalade, Grape (51580)	1954-68, 1978-78	$15-17
1950/4768	2 Tier Tid Bit, 9" and 12 1/2" Plates, Grape (no picture)	1950	$*
1950/123	Toast and Clear Cover, 8" Cupped Plate (see photo, p. 84)	1954-55	$95-110

1950 899
Covered Marmalade

Hobnail

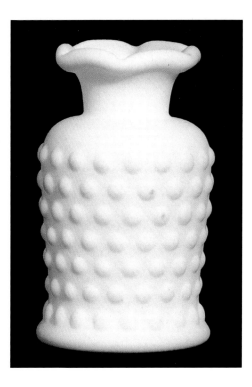

1950/746, 4 1/4"
Crimped Vase, Hobnail.
$12-15.

1950/188 Footed Ivy Bowl, Hobnail. The Ivy Bowl is another item that Imperial made in various colors. A collection of ivy bowls makes a wonderful window display. $25-27.

1950/741 Dresser, 3 Piece Set, Hobnail. *Imperial Glass Photograph.* $85-90.

Catalog Illustrations

1950/630   8 oz. Goblet, Hobnail   1956-60 $10-12
1950/630   6 oz. Sherbet, Hobnail   1956-60 $10-12
1950/630   12 oz Ice Tea, Hobnail   1956-60 $12-15
1950/630   6 oz. Juice, Hobnail   1956-60 $10-12

1950/640   4 1/2" Bowl, Hobnail (51680)   1957-59, 1977-78 $8-10
1950/641   8 1/2" Nappy, Hobnail (51696)   1958-59, 1977-78 $15-20
1950/642   10" Bowl, Hobnail (51700)   1957-59, 1977-78 $20-22

1950/630
8-oz. Goblet

1950/630
6-oz. Sherbet

1950/630
12-oz. Ice Tea

1950/640
4½" Bowl

1950/630
6-oz. Juice

1950/641
8½" Bowl

1950/630   10 oz. Tumbler, Hobnail   1956-60 $12-15
1950/624   54 oz. Pitcher, Hobnail   1956-59 $45-50
1950/638   8" Plate, Hobnail   1956-60 $8-10

1950/630
10-oz. Tumbler

1950/624
54 oz. Pitcher

1950/642
10" Bowl

1950/638
8" Plate

1950/66C   5 1/2" Crimped Bon Bon, Hobnail
         (51720)   1950-71,
                                        1977-78 $18-20
1950/270   Candy Jar & Cover, Hobnail (51876)   1957-65
                                        1977-78 $25-30
1950/615   Footed Box and Cover, Hobnail   1964-68 $30-35
1950/615   Footed Box and Cover, Hobnail
         (Colored Bowl)   1962-62 $40-45

1950/635
Candy Box & Cover

11/742C   7 in. Compote

1950/66C
5½" Crimped Bon Bon

1950 270
Candy Jar & Cover

1950/96   Salt and Pepper, Hobnail
         Glossy Only (51480)   1977-78 $15-20
1950/631   Footed Sugar & Cream Set, Hobnail   1957-60 $22-25
1950/285   Single Candleholder, Hobnail   1956-60 $10-12
1950/643   4" Candleholder (51783), Hobnail   1977-77 $20-22

1950/615
Ftd. Hobnail Box & Cover

Mustard

51480
Salt & Pepper Set

1950/96   Salt and Pepper, Hobnail

51783
4" Candleholder

1950/188   6 1/2" Footed Ivy Bowl, Hobnail
         (11/472N)   1943,
                                      1950-64 $25-27
1950/635   Candy Box and Cover, Hobnail   1956-60 $20-25
11/742C   7" Compote, Hobnail (51720)   1930, 1943,
                                      1977-78 $18-20

1950/631
Footed Sugar & Cream Set

1950 188
6½" Footed Ivy Ball

1950/285
Candleholder

11/742	6 Piece Dresser Set, Hobnail	1932	$85-90
11/742	Box and Cover, Hobnail	1932	$28-30
11/742	Cologne and Stopper, Hobnail	1932	$28-30
1950/741	3 Piece Dresser Set, Hobnail	1956-62	$85-90
1950/743	Box and Cover, Hobnail	1955-62	$28-30
1950/744	Cologne and Stopper, Hobnail	1955-62	$28-30

1950/270	Candy Jar and Cover, Hobnail	1958-62	$25-30
1950/7227	3 Piece Dresser Set, Hobnail	1958-62	$105-120
1950/7243/1	Bottle and Stopper, Hobnail	1958-62	$30-35

742
6-pc. Dresser Set, Hobnail
5 in. Round Puff Box and Cover
Cologne with Stopper

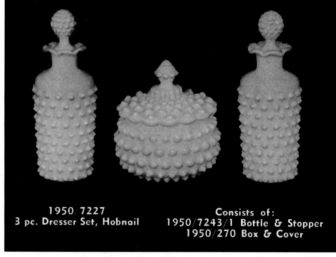

1950/7227
3 pc. Dresser Set, Hobnail

Consists of:
1950/7243/1 Bottle & Stopper
1950/270 Box & Cover

1950/741
3-pc. Dresser Set
Consists of: 1950/744
Cologne & Stopper
1950/743 Box & Cover

| 1950/114 | 7 1/4" Vase Glossy, Hobnail (51762) | 1977-78 | $27-30 |
| 1950/742 | 8" Vase, Hobnail | 1953-55 | $30-35 |

51762
7¼" Lamp Vase

1950/114
7 1/4" Lamp Vase
Glossy Hobnail (51762)

1950/742
8" Hobnail Vase

1950/746	4 1/4" Crimp Vase, Hobnail (51750)	1956-59, 1972-78	$12-15
1950/7243	6" Vase, Hobnail	1957-66	$18-20
11/7423	7 1/2" Blown Vase, Hobnail	1930s	$30-35

1950/746
4¼" Crimped Vase

1950 7243
6" Vase

11/7423C   7 1/2" Blown Vase, Hobnail

Lace Edge and "Lace Edge Cut"

1950/271-273, 3 Piece Heart, 5", 6" and 7", Lace Edge.
Imperial Glass Photograph. $20-25 each.

1950/274C, 7" 4-Toed
Comporte, Lace Edge. $15-20.

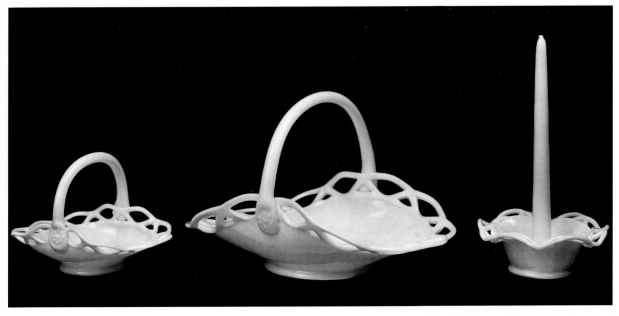

1950/1723, 7 3/4"
Basket, Lace Edge.
$30-35. Also
shown is the larger
1950/1725 Basket,
12 1/2", Lace
Edge, $40-45.
*Imperial Glass
Photograph.*

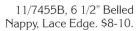

11/7455B, 6 1/2" Belled
Nappy, Lace Edge. $8-10.

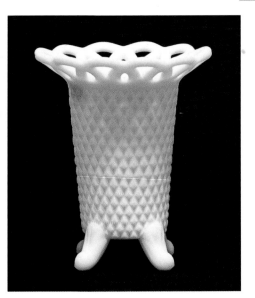

1950/286B, 5" 4-Toed Vase. These vases
were designed with four different collars.
Look closely at the catalog illustrations in
the Lace Edge section. $20-22.

1950/360F, 10"
Footed Fruit Bowl,
"Lace Edge Cut."
This pattern was
made for a short
period only and
not much of it is
seen on the
market. Since it
also does not
seem to have
much demand,
the prices are not
too high. There
are only eleven
accessory pieces
available. $35-40.

Catalog Illustrations — Lace Edge

1950/207C	7 1/2" Crimped Bowl, Lace Edge	1953-65	$8-10
1950/207F	8" Bowl, Lace Edge (11/7566F, 7")	1930s,	
		1953-65	$8-10
1950/275F	10" Bowl, Lace Edge	1953-66	$17-20
1950/745F	6" Bowl, Lace Edge	1953-68	$8-10
1950/745C	6" Crimped Bowl, Lace Edge	1953-68	$8-10

1950/220C
10" Footed Crimped Bowl

1950/207C
7½" Crimped Bowl

1950 745F
6" Bowl

1950 207F
8" Bowl

1950/745C
6" Crimped Bowl

1950 220F
10" Footed Fruit Bowl

1950 275F
10" Bowl

1950/220X
9½" Ftd. Bowl

11/7455G	6" Basket Bowl, Lace Edge	1932	$10-15
11/7455B	6 1/2" Belled Nappy, Lace Edge	1932	$8-10
1950/220C	10" Footed Crimped Bowl, Lace Edge	1957-60	$20-25
1950/220F	10" Footed Fruit Bowl, Lace Edge	1950-71	$25-30
1950/220X	9 1/2" Footed Bowl, Lace Edge	1951-52	$15-20
1950/215	3 Partitioned Relish, Lace Edge	1955-55	$25-30

11/7455G
6" Basket Bowl

11/7455B
6 1/2" Belled Nappy

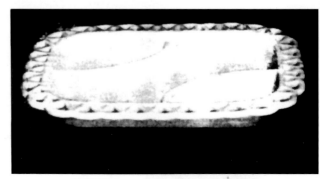

1950/215   3 Partitioned Relish

1950/30	Sugar and Cream Set, Lace Edge	1950-50,		1950/78	9 1/2" Footed Jar, Lace Edge	1962-62	$20-25
		1955-60	$20-25	1950/78C	6" Candleholder, Lace Edge	1956-60	$10-12
1950/790	Sugar and Cream Set, Lace Edge	1955-58	$18-20	1950/220D	12" Footed Cake Stand, Lace Edge	1950-71	$25-30
1950/271	5" Heart, Lace Edge	1959-62	$20-25	1950/220E	12" Footed Banana Stand,		
1950/272	6" Heart, Lace Edge	1959-62	$20-25		Lace Edge	1950-68	$30-35
1950/273	7" Heart, Lace Edge	1959-62	$20-25	1950/715	Pie Server, Lace Edge (no picture)	1954-55	$*
1950/207K	5" Flower Arranger	1965-69	$15-20				

1950/30
Sugar & Cream Set

1950/790
Sugar & Cream Set

1950/207K
5" Flower Arranger

1950/78
9 1/2" Footed Jar,
Lace Edge

1950/78C
6" Lace Edge Candleholder

1950 271
5" Lace Edge Heart

1950/272
6" Lace Edge Heart

1950 273
7" Lace Edge Heart

1950 220D
12" Footed Cake Stand

1950 220E
12" Footed Banana Bowl

1950/274C	7" 4-Toed Compote, Lace Edge	1953-65	$15-20
1950/749B	7" Comporte, Lace Edge	1954-60	$12-15
1950/749F	7" Comporte, Lace Edge	1954-66	$12-15
1950/749F	7" Comporte With Brass Handle, Lace Edge	1962-62	$25-30
1950/1723	7 3/4" Basket, Lace Edge	1956-60	$30-35
1950/1725	12 1/2" or 13" Basket, Lace Edge	1956-60	$40-45
1950/286B	5" Vase 4-Toed, Lace Edge	1953-62	$20-22
11/743B	5 1/4" Vase, Lace Edge	1930s	$12-15
11/743K	5" Vase, Lace Edge	1930s	$12-15
11/743N	5 1/2" Vase, Lace Edge	1930s	$12-15
11/743X	4 1/2" Vase, Lace Edge	1930s	$12-15
11/7455D	7 1/2" Plate, Lace Edge	1932	$8-10

1950/274C
7" 4-Toed Comporte

1950/749B
7" Lace Edge Comporte

1950/286B
5" 4-Toed Vase

11/743B   5 1/4" Vase

1950/749F
7" Lace Edge Comporte

Milk Glass
1950/749F

11/743K
5" Vase

11/743N
5 1/2" Vase

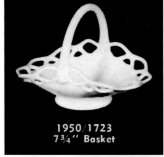

1950/1723
7 3/4" Basket

11/743X
4 1/2" Vase

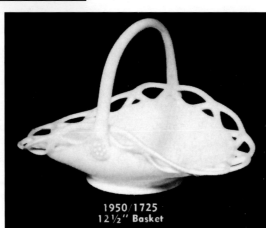

1950/1725
12 1/2" Basket

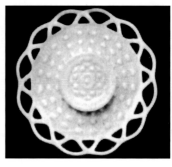

11/7455D
7 1/2" Plate

Catalog Illustrations — "Lace Edge, Cut"

1950/360D 12" Footed Cake Stand,
     "Lace Edge Cut"   1956-60 $30-35
1950/360E 12" Footed Banana Bowl,
     "Lace Edge Cut"   1956-60 $35-40
1950/360F 10" Footed Fruit Bowl,
     "Lace Edge Cut"   1956-60 $35-40

1950/361F
10" Bowl

1950/360D
12" Footed Cake Stand

1950/362F
8" Bowl

1950/363F
6" Bowl

1950/360E
12" Footed Banana Bowl

1950/364F
7" Comporte

1950/365B
7" 4-Toed Comporte

1950/360F
10" Footed Fruit Bowl

1950/366C
6" Candleholder

1950/367
7¾" Basket

1950/361F   10" Bowl, "Lace Edge Cut"   1956-60 $25-30
1950/362F   8" Bowl, "Lace Edge Cut"   1956-60 $20-25
1950/363F   6" Bowl, "Lace Edge Cut"   1956-60 $15-20
1950/364F   7" Comporte, "Lace Edge Cut"   1956-60 $15-17
1950/365B   7" 4-Toed Comporte, "Lace Edge Cut" 1956-60 $15-17
1950/366C   6" Candleholder, "Lace Edge Cut"   1956-60 $15-17
1950/367   7 3/4" Basket, "Lace Edge Cut"   1956-60 $35-40
1950/368   12 1/2" Basket, "Lace Edge Cut"   1956-60 $40-50

1950/368
12½" Basket

"Leaf" and "Leaf Open"

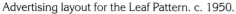

M. G. 1979

Advertising layout for the Leaf Pattern. c. 1950.

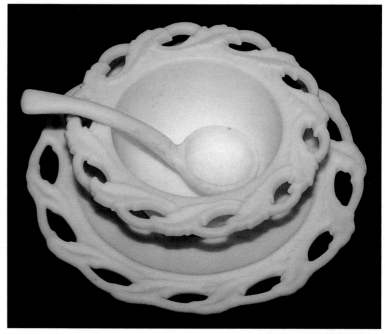

1950/818 3-Piece Mayonnaise Set, "Leaf, Open." The "Leaf" and "Leaf, Open" patterns were made for three and five years respectively. Both are limited patterns. Collectors may find stems and plates as well as accessories items in the "Leaf" pattern. $25-30 set.

Catalog Illustrations — "Leaf"

1950/700	9 oz. Goblet, "Leaf"	1952-55	$12-15
1950/700	6 oz. Sherbet, "Leaf"	1952-55	$12-15
1950/700	5 1/2 oz. Footed Juice, "Leaf"	1952-55	$12-15
1950/700	12 oz. Footed Ice Tea, "Leaf"	1952-55	$15-20
1950/164	9 oz. Luncheon Goblet, "Leaf"	1950-50	$15-20
1950/164	6 oz. Luncheon Sherbet, "Leaf"	1950-50	$15-20
1950/703D	7" Plate, "Leaf"	1952-55	$8-10
1950/705D	8 1/2" Plate, "Leaf"	1952-55	$10-12
1950/710D	10 1/2" Plate, "Leaf"	1952-55	$15-18
1950/723	3 Piece Mayonnaise Set, "Leaf"	1952-55	$25-30

1950/700
9 oz. Goblet

1950/700
6 oz. Sherbet

1950/700
5 1/2 oz. Footed Juice

1950/700
12 oz. Footed Ice Tea

1950/164
9 oz. Luncheon Goblet

1950/164
6 oz. Luncheon Sherbet

1950/703D
7" Plate

1950/705D
8½" Plate

1950/710D
10½" Plate

1950/737
Cup and Saucer

1950/723
3 pc. Mayonnaise Set

1950/752
6½" Fruit

1950/759
6½" Candy Box
and Cover

1950/730	Sugar and Cream Set, "Leaf"	1952-55	$22-25
1950/737	Cup and Saucer, "Leaf"	1952-55	$15-17
1950/752	6 1/2" Fruit, "Leaf"	1952-55	$8-10
1950/759	6 1/2" Candy Box and Cover, "Leaf"	1952-55	$15-17
1950/765	9" Candy Box and Cover, "Leaf"	1952-55	$20-25

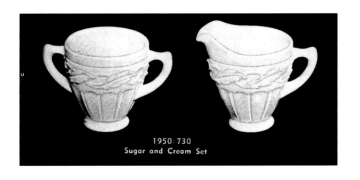

1950/730
Sugar and Cream Set

1950/765
9" Candy Box and Cover

1950/766	11" Float Bowl With 3 Candle		
	Sockets, "Leaf"	1952-55	$20-22
1950/767D	10" Cake Stand, "Leaf"	1952-55	$30-35
1950/767X	11" Footed Fruit Bowl, "Leaf"	1952-55	$35-40
1950/775X	9" Bowl, "Leaf"	1952-55	$22-25
1950/780	3 1/2" Low Candleholder, "Leaf"	1952-55	$15-17

Catalog Illustrations — "Leaf Open"

1950/785	6 1/2" Candy Box and Cover,		
	"Leaf Open"	1955-60	$18-20
1950/817	11 1/4" Fruit Bowl, "Leaf Open"	1956-60	$25-30
1950/786	6 1/2" Bowl, "Leaf Open"	1955-60	$8-10
1950/815	9" Candy Box and Cover, "Leaf Open"	1955-60	$25-30
1950/816	9" Bowl, "Leaf Open"	1955-60	$18-20
1950/818	3 Piece Mayo, "Leaf Open"	1956-60	$25-30
1950/840	11" Candle Float, "Leaf Open"	1956-62	$28-30

1950/817
11¼" Fruit Bowl

1950/786
6½" Bowl

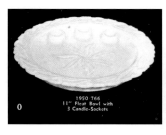

1950-766
11" Float Bowl with
3 Candle-Sockets

1950/767D
13" Cake Stand

1950/815
9" Candy Box & Cover

1950 767X
11" Footed Fruit Bowl

1950 775X
9" Bowl

1950/816
9" Bowl

1950/780
3½" Low Candleholder

1950/818
3-pc. Mayonnaise Set

1950/785
6½" Candy Box & Cover

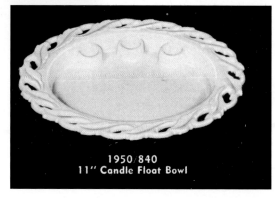

1950/840
11" Candle Float Bowl

Rose

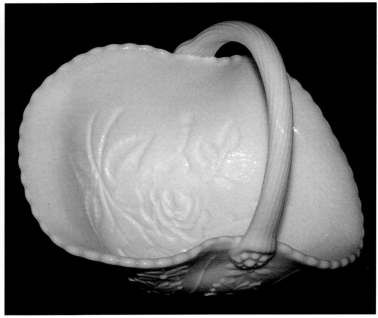

1950/161, 8" Covered Butter or Cheese, Rose. $35-38.

1950/489, 8" Basket. The 1950/489 Basket was exciting to find. With no catalog illustration to follow, we did not realize it belonged in the Rose pattern. The basket has daisies on the exterior, while the interior design is an open rose similar to the 1950/10D Rose Plate. $35-40.

Catalog Illustrations

1950/10D	10 1/2" Wall or Buffet Plate, Rose	1950-71	$15-20
1950/13D	12 1/2" Torte or Wall Plate, Rose	1950-64	$20-22

1950/62C	9" Crimped Bowl, Rose (51699)	1950-71, 1977-78	$20-22
1950/74	3-Toed Bowl, Rose (51690)	1952-59, 1977-78	$22-25
1950/113C	11 1/2" 3-Toed Crimped Fruit, Rose	1950-69	$30-35

1950/10D
10 1/2" Wall or Buffet Plate, Rose

1950/489	8" Basket (see photo, p. 111)	1968-69	$35-40
1950/489	9 oz. Tumbler, Rose	1950-50	$10-12
1950/24	3 Pint Water Pitcher, Rose	1950-50	$35-40
1950/249	9 Piece Water Set, Rose	1950-50	$115-140

1950/108
6" Vase, Rose

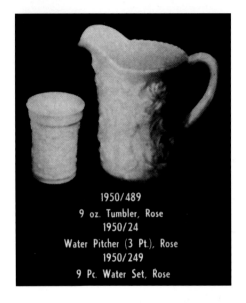

1950/489
9 oz. Tumbler, Rose
1950/24
Water Pitcher (3 Pt.), Rose
1950/249
9 Pc. Water Set, Rose

1950/116
6" Vase

1950/25	Covered Sugar, Rose	1950-60	$15-20
1950/26	Cream Pitcher, Rose	1950-60	$15-20
1950/2526	Covered Sugar and Cream Set, Rose	1950-60	$30-40
1950/161	8" Covered Butter or Cheese, Rose	1950-64	$35-38
1950/108	6" Vase, Rose (51751)	1953-70, 1978-78	$15-17
1950/116	6" Vase, Rose	1956-60	$15-18
1950/181	6 1/4" Vase, Rose	1955-68	$22-25
1950/160	3 1/2" Candleholder, Rose	1955-71	$10-12

1950/181
6¼" Vase, Rose

1950/2526
Sugar & Cream Set
Consists of:
1950/25 Sugar & Cover
1950/26 Cream Pitcher

1950/160
3½" Candleholder

1950/161
8" Covered Butter or Cheese

Scroll

1950/772 Sugar and Cream Set, Scroll. $20-25.

1950/236/1 Candleholder, Scroll. $15-20 each.

Catalog Illustrations

1950/3226	7" Bread and Butter Plate, Scroll	1956-60	$6-8
1950/3227	8" Plate, Scroll	1956-60	$6-8
1950/3228	8 3/4" Plate, Scroll	1956-60	$8-10
1950/3229	9 3/4" Plate, Scroll	1956-60	$10-12
1950/321	60 oz. Pitcher, Scroll	1955-60	$45-50

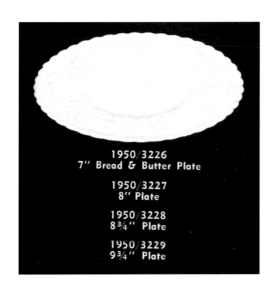

1950/3226
7" Bread & Butter Plate

1950/3227
8" Plate

1950/3228
8¾" Plate

1950/3229
9¾" Plate

1950/321
60-oz. Pitcher

1950/322	11 oz. Goblet, Scroll	1956-60	$10-12
1950/322	7 oz. Sherbet, Scroll	1956-60	$10-12
1950/322	6 oz. Juice, Scroll	1956-60	$10-12
1950/322	5 oz. Wine, Scroll	1956-60	$10-12
1950/322	10 oz. Tumbler, Scroll	1956-60	$10-12
1950/322	12 oz. Ice Tea, Scroll	1955-60	$10-12

1950/329	3-Toed Bowl, Scroll	1956-60	$12-15
1950/120	Bridesmaid's Bowl, Scroll	1952-62	$25-27
1950/120C	5 1/2" Footed Crimped Bowl, Scroll	1958-62	$20-25
1950/125	Wedding Bowl and Cover, Scroll	1953-61	$35-40
1950/236/1	Candleholder, Scroll (see photo, p. 113)	1958-60	$15-20
1950/396	Salt and Pepper Set, Scroll	1956-60	$18-20
1950/3235	Cup and Saucer, Scroll	1956-60	$15-20

1950/322
11-oz. Goblet

1950/322
7-oz. Sherbet

1950/322
6-oz. Juice

1950/329
3-Toed Bowl

1950 120
Bridesmaid's Bowl & Cover

1950/322
5-oz. Wine

1950/322
10-oz. Tumbler

1950/322
12-oz. Ice Tea

1950/120C
5½" Footed Crimped Bowl

1950/235	8" Berry Bowl, Scroll	1955-60	$15-20
1950/236	5" Nappy, Scroll	1955-60	$10-12
1950/332	4" Square Bowl, Scroll	1957-60	$10-12
1950/331	3 Piece Mayonnaise Set, Scroll	1957-60	$20-32
1950/333	Mayo Plate, Scroll, (same as in 1950/331)	1957-60	$8-10

1950/125
Bowl and Cover

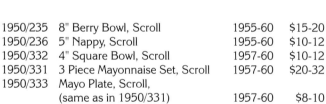

1950/235
8" Berry Bowl

1950/236
5" Nappy

1950/396
Salt & Pepper Set

1950/331
3-pc. Mayonnaise Set

1950/332
4" Square Bowl

1950/3235
Cup and Saucer

1950/772	Sugar and Cream Set, Scroll	1955-60	$20-25
1950/342	Puff Box and Cover, Scroll	1956-58	$35-40
1950/209	Cologne Bottle and Stopper, Scroll	1956-58	$35-40
1950/3412	3 Piece Dresser Set, Scroll	1956-58	$105-120

1950/772
Sugar & Cream Set

1950/3412
3-pc. Dresser Set Consists of:
1950/209 Cologne Bottle &
Stopper and 1950/342 Puff Box
& Cover

Windmill

Catalog Illustrations

1950/58C	9" Crimped Plate, Windmill	1952-55	$18-20
1950/52C	8" Crimped Bowl, Windmill	1950-60	$20-22
1950/58D	9 1/2" Oval Plate, Windmill	1952-55	$20-22
1950/58A	8" Oval Bowl, Windmill	1952-55	$18-20

1950/240, 1 Pint Milk Pitcher. $30-35.

1950/58C
9" Crimped Plate

1950/58D
9½" Oval Plate

1950/52C
8" Crimped Dinette Bowl, Windmill

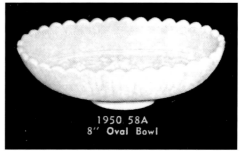

1950/58A
8" Oval Bowl

1950/7D	9" Wall or Luncheon Plate, Windmill	1950-60	$15-20
1950/239	Pitcher 3 Pint, Windmill (Pictured in Set)	1950-52	$45-50
1950/240	Milk Pitcher 1 Pint, Windmill	1950-65	$30-35
1950/269	9 Piece Water Set, Windmill	1950-52	$125-135
1950/514	9 oz. Tumbler, Windmill	1950-52	$12-15

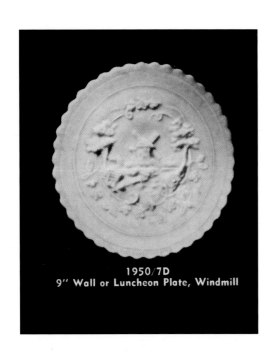

1950/7D
9" Wall or Luncheon Plate, Windmill

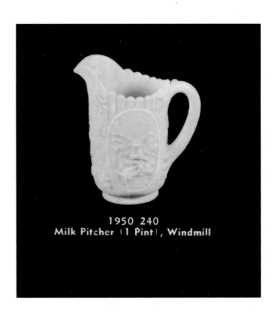

1950 240
Milk Pitcher (1 Pint), Windmill

1950/269
9 pc. Water Set, Windmill
Consists of:
(1—1950/239 Pitcher,
8—1950/514 9 oz. Tumblers)

Categories—Photographs and Catalog Illustrations

Animals and Animal Related

1950/146, 4 1/2" Duck-on-Nest. $30-35.

1950/149, 5 1/2" Turkey -on-Nest, red painted comb. $35-40.

1950/147, 4" Swan Mint Whimsy. $20-25. The design on the neck of the Imperial Swan Whimsy, 1950/147, resembles feathers. In contrast, the design on the neck of the 4" Swan made by Fenton Art Glass Company is comprised of dots. It would be nice if you could remember these designs by associating Fenton with feathers, but in this case it is the opposite: Imperial has feathers and Fenton has dots! We learned this lesson in association from Mr. Frank Fenton when we were fortunate enough to have lunch with him during the 1991 NIGCS convention.

1950/149, 5 1/2" Turkey-on-Nest, not painted. $35-40.

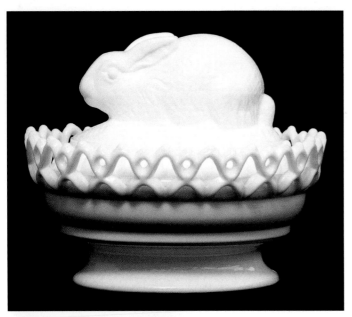

1950/157 "Rabbit" Box and Cover. Hard to find. $250-300.

1950/158 "Rooster" Box and Cover. $175-200.

1950/162 Bunny-on-Nest (11/162). $25-30.

Advertising Mat for the Parlor Pups. c. 1950

1950/148, 4 1/2" Swan-on Nest. The Swan-on-Nest is more difficult to find than the other small covered dishes. $30-35.

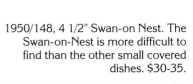

1950/500 "Parlor Puppy," or "Parlor Pups" as they are more commonly called, are rather hard to find. Two of the four have not been found yet by us. $35-40 each.

1950/777 Eagle Book End. The milk glass eagle has not joined the flock of crystal, satin, and gold eagles in our collection. Pictured here is a satin finished eagle so that you may see the details. $*

Catalog Illustrations

1950/134	Hobby Horse Cigarette Box	1950-50	$*
1950/145	4 1/2" Hen-On-Nest (11/145)	1930s, 1943	$25-30
1950/145	4 1/2" Hen-On Nest	1950-71, 1977-78	$25-30
1950/146	4 1/2" Duck-On-Nest	1952-60	$30-35

1950/157
"Rabbit" Box & Cover

1950/134
Hobby Horse Cigarette Box
Available only with Decoration
or Doeskin Finish

1950 145
4 1/2" Hen-on-Nest

1950/158	"Rooster" Box and Cover	1957-69	$175-200
1950/159	Atterbury Lion Box and Cover	1959-60	$225-250
1950/162	Bunny-On-Nest (11/162) (51923)	1943, 1950-70, 1977-78	$25-30

1950/145
4 1/2" Hen-on-Nest

1950/146
4 1/2" Duck-on-Nest

1950/147	4" Swan Mint Whimsy (11/147)	1943, 1950-71	$20-25
1950/148	4 1/2" Swan-On-Nest	1951-60	$30-35
1950/149	5 1/2" Turkey-On-Nest (red painted comb on some)	1952-60	$35-40
1950/154	Bird Box and Cover	1959-59	$*
1950/155	Rabbit-On-Nest	1953-58	$200-225
1950/157	"Rabbit" Box and Cover	1957-60	$250-300

1950 158
"Rooster" Box & Cover

1950/147
Swan Mint Whimsy

1950/148
4 1/2" Swan-on-Nest

1950/149
5 1/2" Turkey-on-Nest

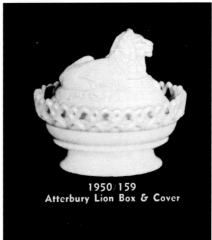

1950/159
Atterbury Lion Box & Cover

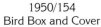

1950/154
Bird Box and Cover

1950/155
Covered Rabbit

1950/162
4" Bunny-on-Nest

1950/214	Atterbury Dove Box and Cover	1957-60	$175-200
1950/400	8" Swan	1953-66	$35-40
1950/800	Owl Jar and Cover	1955-60	$80-85
1950/459	Cocktail Pick, Cigarette Holder, Egg Cup, Rooster	1957-60	$25-30
1950/777	Eagle Book End	1955-55	$*
1950/500	4 Piece "Parlor Puppy" Set	1952-52	$140-160

1950/459
Cocktail Pick or Cigarette Holder or Egg Cup

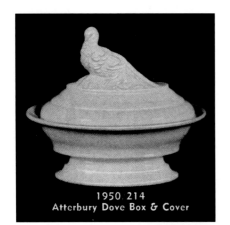

1950 214
Atterbury Dove Box & Cover

1950 400
8" Swan

Eagle Book End (shown in satin finish)

1950/800
Owl Jar & Cover

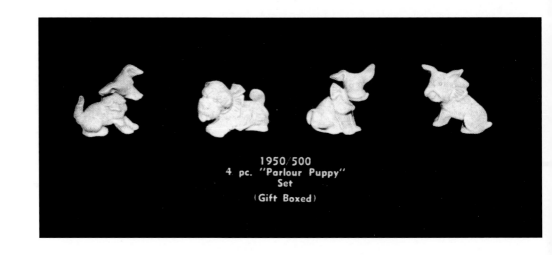

1950/500
4 pc. "Parlour Puppy"
Set
(Gift Boxed)

120

Baskets

Catalog Illustrations

1950/40	9 1/2" Basket, Daisy	1950-64	$30-35
1950/73	5" Pansy Basket	1952-69	$20-25
1950/156	5 1/2" Basket	1968-71	$18-20
1950/221	8" Oval Basket	1955-60	$25-30
1950/252	13 1/2" Large Handled Basket	1951-55	$25-27
1950/435	6" Partitioned Basket (no picture)	1959-60	$*
1950/475	Miniature Basket	1959-64	$15-20

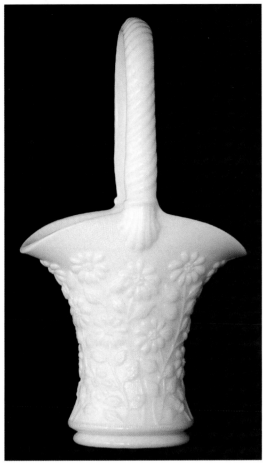

1950/40, 9 1/2" Daisy Basket. $30-35.

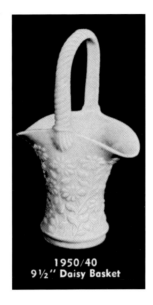

1950/40
9½" Daisy Basket

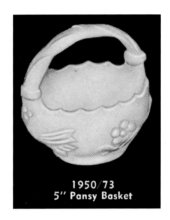

1950/73
5" Pansy Basket

1950/156 — 5-1/2"
Basket

1950/221
8" Oval Basket

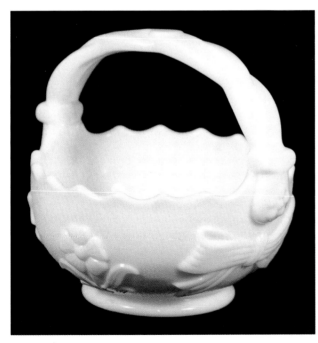

1950/73, 5" Pansy Basket. $20-25.

1950 475
Miniature Basket

1950/252
13½" Large Handled Basket

Bowls, Plates, and Trays

1950/85, 14" Oblong Tray. $22-25.

1950/92, 9 1/2" 3-Toed Bowl. $25-28.

Catalog Illustrations

1950/23B	5 1/2" Dessert Bowl, Open Border	1950-50	$6-8
1950/69	6" Square Bowl	1952-60	$15-17
1950/72	12" x 9 1/2" Salad or Dessert Bowl	1951-52	$25-30
1950/92	9 1/2" 3-Toed Bowl	1951-52	$25-28
1950/860	Footed Bowl & Cover, 9 1/2" Tall	1956-60	$30-35

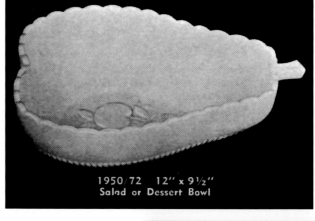

1950/72 12" x 9½"
Salad or Dessert Bowl

1950/23B
5½ in. Open Border Cute Dessert

1950/69
6" Bowl

1950/860
Bowl & Cover, 9½" Tall

1950/92
9½" 3-Toed Bowl

1950/159/1	7 3/4" Atterbury Bowl	1959-69	$45-50
1950/203F	8 1/4" Fruit Bowl	1955-64	$25-30
1950/217	Hawaiian Server 5 1/2" x 11",		
	Pineapple	1950-52	$22-25
1950/463	10" Oval Bowl "Beaded Rib"	1958-64	$30-35
1950/464	8 1/4" Deep Bowl, "Daisy"	1958-62	$30-35

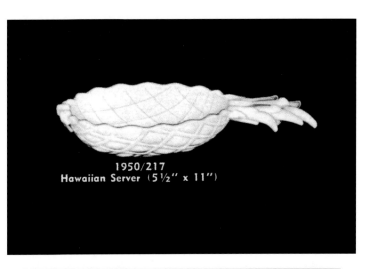

1950/217
Hawaiian Server (5½" x 11")

1950/159/1
7¾" Atterbury Bowl

1950/463
10" Oval Bowl
"Beaded Rib"

1950 203F
8¼" Fruit Bowl

1950/464
8¼" Deep Bowl
"Daisy"

1950/5D	8" Salad or Wall Plate, Open Border	1950-50	$8-10
1950/465	9 1/2" Footed Oblong Bowl, "Chain Edge"	1958-62	$28-30
1950/23D	7 1/2" Bread and Butter, Open Border	1950-50	$6-8
1950/68D	10 1/2" Pastry Tray	1950-50	$20-22
1950/85	14" Oblong Tray	1952-60	$22-25
1950/275D	12" Snack Plate (no picture)	1953-55	$*
1950/297	7 1/2" Shell Tray	1951-58	$12-15
1950/524	10 1/2" Buffet or Wall Plate, Mum	1950-60	$28-30
1950/525	10 1/2" Buffet or Wall Plate, Homestead	1950-60	$28-30
1950/131	Festive Bowl and Cover	1952-55	$30-32
1950/131B	7 1/4" x 7 1/4" Footed Bowl	1952-55	$20-22
1950/717	10" Wall Plate Fruit (no picture)	1954-55	$*

1950/68D
10½ in. Pastry Tray

1950/85
14" Oblong Tray

1950/5D
8 in. Open Border Salad or Wall Plate

1950/297
7½" Shell Tray

1950/524
10½" Buffet or Wall Plate, Mum

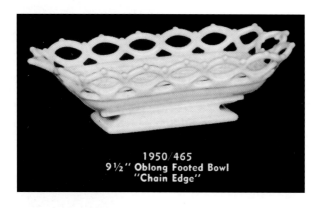

1950/465
9½" Oblong Footed Bowl
"Chain Edge"

1950/525
10½" Buffet or Wall Plate,
Homestead

1950/131
Festive Bowl & Cover
(Weddings, Anniversaries, etc.)

1950/23D
7½ in. Open Border Bread
and Butter Plate

1950/131B
7¼" x 7¼" Footed Bowl

Candy and Cake Stands

1950/495 Candy Jar and Cover, "Parakeet." $70-75.

1950/462 Candy Box and Cover. $30-35.

Catalog Illustrations

1950/65	Oblong Candy Box and Cover	1955-58	$35-40
1950/110	10 1/2" 1-lb. Covered Candy	1950-55	$15-20
1950/133	1-lb. Footed Candy and Cover	1950-52	$30-35
1950/140	Candy Jar and Cover, Pineapple	1951-52	$40-45

1950/65
Oblong Candy Box & Cover

1950/133   1-lb.
Footed Candy Jar and Cover

1950/110   10½"
1-lb. Covered Candy Jar

1950/140
Pineapple Candy Jar and Cover

1950/199	8" Shell Float Candy or Relish	1950-52	$12-15
1950/203D	10" Cake Stand	1955-60	$25-30
1950/259	Candy Box and Cover	1952-60	$22-25
1950/260	"Watch" Candy Box and Cover	1958-60	$65-70

1950/310	1-lb. Shenadoah Apple Candy Jar and Cover (no picture)	1951-51	$*
1950/311	1-lb. Pear Candy Jar and Cover, Beaded Block	1951-52	$*
1950/311	Pitcher, Beaded Block (no picture)	1951-52	$*
1950/311	Vase, Beaded Block (no picture)	1951-52	$*
1950/312	6" Candy Box, Heart Shape	1951-52	$25-30
1950/425	1-lb. Footed Candy and Cover	1950-64	$22-25
1950/456	7 1/2" Handled Candy Box & Cover	1957-60	$20-25
1950/458	Footed Covered Candy, Fleur-De-Lis	1958-60	$28-30
1950/460	Coach Lamp Candy Box & Cover	1957-59	$40-45
1950/461	Oblong, Footed, Eagle Finial, Candy Box	1958-60	$60-65
1950/462	Candy Box and Cover	1957-60	$30-35

1950/199 8"
Shell Float Candy or Relish

1950/203D
10" Cake Stand

1950/311 1-lb.
Pear Candy Jar & Cover

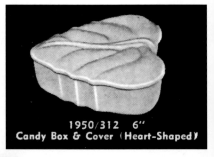

1950/312 6"
Candy Box & Cover (Heart-Shaped)

1950 259
Candy Box and Cover

1950 260
"Watch" Candy Box & Cover

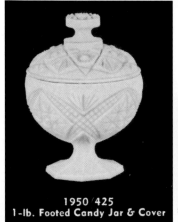

1950 425
1-lb. Footed Candy Jar & Cover

1950 456
Handled Candy Box & Cover

1950/458
Footed Candy Box & Cover
"Fleur de Lis"

1950/460
"Coach Lamp" Candy Box & Cover

461
"Eagle"
Box and Cover

1950/462
Candy Box & Cover

1950 973
Candy Box & Cover

1950/495	Candy Jar and Cover, "Parakeet"	1958-60	$70-75
1950/911	Candy Box and Cover (no picture)	1959-60	$*
1950/972	Candy Box and Cover	1960-62	$35-40
1950/973	Candy Box, Footed and Cover	1959-62	$25-30
1950/974	Footed Candy Box & Cover (51934)	1961-64, 1977-78	$30-35
1950/975	Candy Box and Cover	1961-69	$25-30
1950/976	Footed Candy Box and Cover	1961-69	$25-30
11/699	Tall Footed Candy Jar, Washington	1943-43	$40-45

51934
Baltimore
Pear Jar & Cover

1950/974
Footed Candy Box
and Cover

1950/975
Candy Box & Cover

1950/495
Candy Jar & Cover
"Parakeet"

1950/976
Ftd. Candy Box & Cover

1950 972
Candy Box & Cover

11/699 - Tall Ftd.
Candy Jar & Cover

Candleholders and Lamps

1950/80, 7 1/2" Vinelf Candleholder. $25-30.

1950/9 Bundling Lamp. $90-100.

1950/201 Lamp Peacock Feather, Milk Glass with Antique Blue. This lamp can also be found in all Antique Blue. Other colors and combinations are Amber and Mustard (yellow). $100-125.

1950/9 Bundling Lamp with Ruby Shade. The Bundling Lamp came in many colors and combinations of colors, however the milk glass with ruby shade is the one most often found. Prices for colors and combinations vary, ranging from $50 for Amber, $90 for Milk Glass, and $125 for Ultra Blue in the solid colors, and $75 for combinations.

"Vinelf Comport and Matching Candleholders" POPA Tag. The inside reads: "Truly a collector's item is this hand-crafted Cherub of the Vineyard! This handsome piece derives its inspiration from an old compote designed long ago by Thomas Atterbury—a foremost fashioner of glass in the Pittsburgh area during the 1880s. Ask to see the matching Vinelf Candlesticks! Pressed by hand, of high quality glass, this Provincial styling is genuine Americana and bears the Imperial mark of antique authenticity." On the back of the tag is this notation: "Made in America, of course." Imperial was proud of American glass. The company often used the words American Hand-crafted and House of Americana Glass. After all, it was the largest glass factory under one roof in America.

Catalog Illustrations

1950/80	7 1/2" Vinelf Candleholder	1950-65	$25-30
1950/81	5" Handled Candleholder	1952-59	$10-12
1950/81	5" Footed and Handled Candleholder	1964-69	$12-15

1950/279	Twin Candleholder	1953-64	$10-12
1950/280	4" Candleholder	1950-50	$15-20
1950/325	3 1/4" Candleholder	1955-62	$15-18
1950/330	7" Tall Candleholder (51796)	1955-60, 1977-78	$12-15
1950/779	5" Dolphin Candleholder	1953-60	$15-20

1950/81
5" Handled Candleholder

1950/81
Ftd. Hdld.
Candleholder

1950 80
7½" Vinelf Candleholder

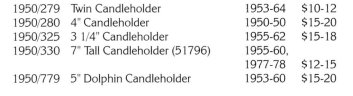

1950/280
4 in. Candleholder

1950/279
Twin Candleholder

1950/325
3¼" Candleholder

1950/330
7" Tall Candleholder

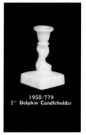

1950/779
5" Dolphin Candleholder

1950/90	8" Dolphin Candleholder (51792)	1954-58, 1977-78	$20-25
1950/100	4" Twin Candleholder	1950-68	$8-10
1950/119	9 1/2" Crucifix Candleholder (11/119)	1943, 1955-55	$80-85

1950 90
8" Dolphin Candleholder

1950 100
4" Twin Candleholder

1950/119 Crucifix (Imperial Photo)

1950/9	Bundling Lamp, Glossy Only	1954-65	$90-100
1950/79	2 Piece Hurricane, 11 1/2", (Crystal Chimney)	1950-50	$40-50
1950/201	Lamp, Peacock Feather, 14"	1962-62	$80-85
1950/201H	Handled Lamp 12"	1962-62	$80-85

1950 9
Bundling Lamp

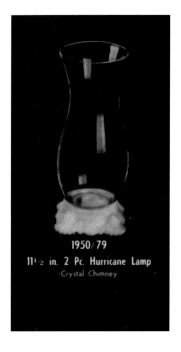

1950/79
11½ in. 2 Pc. Hurricane Lamp
Crystal Chimney

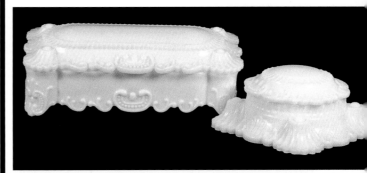

Cigarette Items

1950/201
Lamp Peacock Feather 14"

Milk Glass
1950/201H

1950/350	Handled Lamp 14"	1962-62	$80-85
1950/607	12" Oval Candle Bowl	1957-62	$25-28
1950/5027	2 Piece Hurricane, Cathay	1954-60	$85-95

1950/350
14" Handled Lamp

1950/5027
2-pc. Hurricane Lamp

1950/607
12" Oval Candle Bowl

Opposite page, right side:

Top: Left: 1950/191, 8 1/2" Partitioned Cigarette, Boudoir or Desk Box. Right: 1950/144, 5" Covered Puff, Pin, Desk Box. While these items have been associated with cigarette and desk accessories, Boudoir collectors now seek them for dresser accessory collections. These items are not seen often. Partitioned Box $80-85. 5" Box $35-40.

Center: 1950/150, 4 1/2" Boudoir or Desk Ash Tray. $15-20.

Bottom: 1950/1776 Federal Eagle Ash Tray, 6 1/4". $65-70.

1950/295	6" Acorn Ash Tray	1951-52	$25-30
1950/402	Cigarette Holder	1956-64	$15-18
1950/422	Atlantis Cigarette Box and Cover or Desk Box	1950-55	$45-50
1950/450	4 Piece Trivet Ash Tray Set	1950-64	$35-40
1950/505	Cigarette Holder (41624)	1955-68, 1977-78	$15-20
1950/505	4 Piece Cigarette Set or Toothpick Set (41624)	1978-78	$60-80
1950/520	9 1/2" Zodiac Ash Tray	1956-66	$20-22

Catalog Illustrations

1950/29	5" Fish Ash Tray	1952-52	$20-22
1950/150	4 1/2" Boudoir or Desk Ash Tray	1950-52	$15-20
1950/191	8 1/2" Partitioned Cigarette or Boudoir Box	1950-52	$80-85

**1950/29
5" Ash Tray**

**1950/191 8½"
Partitioned Cigarette, Boudoir or Desk Box**

**1950/150 4½"
Boudoir or Desk Ash Tray**

1950/291	Atlantis (Shell) Ash Tray, Nut or Candy	1950-66	$10-12
1950/292	6 1/4" Double Hand Ash Tray, Nut or Candy	1951-52	$30-35
1950/294	4 1/4" Heart Ash Tray	1951-55	$12-15

**1950/291 4½"
Atlantis Ash Tray, Nut or Candy**

**1950/292
6¼" Double-Hand Ash Tray, Nut or Candy**

**1950/294
4¼" Heart Ash Tray**

**1950/295
6" Acorn Ash Tray**

**1950/402
Cigarette Holder**

**1950/422
Atlantis Cigarette Box & Cover or Desk Box**

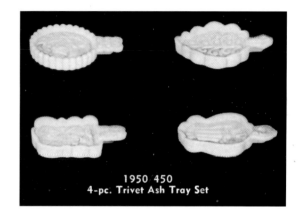

**1950/450
4-pc. Trivet Ash Tray Set**

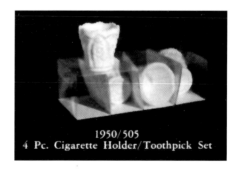

**1950/505
4 Pc. Cigarette Holder/Toothpick Set**

**1950/505
Cigarette Holder**

**1950/520
9½" Zodiac Ash Tray**

1950/532	7" Ash Tray	1959-69	$15-18
1950/758	5" Ash Tray	1959-62	$10-12
1950/776	Federal Footed Cigarette Holder	1952-55	$40-45
1950/801	Cigarette or Tom and Jerry Mug (no picture) (11/592)	1953-55	$20-25
1950/612	4 Piece Toothpick or Cigarette Set	1966-67	$55-60
1950/1776	6 1/4" Federal Eagle Ash Tray	1952-55	$65-70
11/7850	Covered Cigarette Box	1930s	$30-35
11/739	Card or Cigarette Holder, Dog on Side	1930s	$30-35

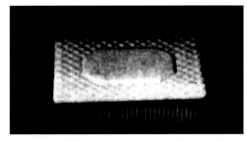

11/7850   Covered Cigarette Box

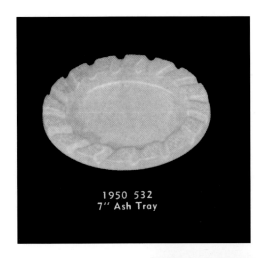

11/739   Card or Cigarette
Holder, Dog on Side

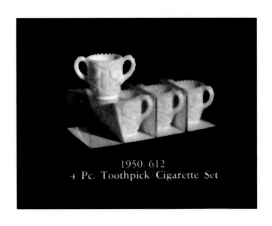

Comportes and Condiments

1950/474C, 7" Comporte. $15-20.

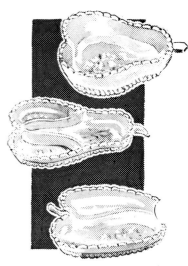

Advertising Mat showing the Pear Shaped Relish Trays.

M. G. 1964

1950/678, 8 1/2" 2 Handled Pickle. $15-18.

Catalog Illustrations

1950/48	7" Centre Comporte	1950-52	$22-25
1950/54	8" Relish, Horseshoe	1956-60	$15-20
1950/55	9" Partitioned Relish, Apple	1951-52	$20-22
1950/56	12" Partitioned Relish, Pear Shape	1951-52	$25-30
1950/67	8 1/2" Fruit Comporte, Vinelf	1950-65	$35-40
1950/474C	7" Comporte	1956-62	$15-20
1950/612	8 1/2" 2 Handled Round Comporte	1958-60	$15-18

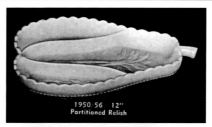

1950/56 12" Partitioned Relish

1950/474C 7" Comporte

1950 67 8½" Vinelf Fruit Comporte

1950/48 7" Centre Comporte

1950/54 8" Relish

1950 55 9" Partitioned Apple Relish

1950/612 8½" 2-Handled Round Comporte

133

1950/613	9" 2 Handled Comporte	1958-60	$15-18
1950/778	7" Dolphin Comporte	1954-60	$25-30
1950/23	3 Piece Mayonnaise, Open Border	1950-50	$20-22
1950/156	4 1/2" Breakfast Marmalade and Cover (11/54)	1930s, 1952-64	$18-20
1950/505/1	6 1/2 oz. Cruet and Stopper	1956-60	$25-30
1950/4021	4 1/2" Footed Jelly	1958-68	$20-22
1950/60	5 1/2" Jar, Gold Decorated, Glossy Only (11/60)	1943, 1950-60	$50-55
1950/567	Pineapple Marmalade Jar and Cover, Spoon	1959-65	$40-45
1950/564	8" Pickle	1958-66	$12-15
1950/678	8 1/2" 2 Handled Pickle	1958-64	$15-18

1950/4021
4½" Footed Jelly

1950 60
5½" Honey or Jam, Decorated Gold
Bees, Ribbon & Base

1950/613
9" 2-Handled Oval Comporte

1950 567
Pineapple Marmalade Jar & Cover

1950/778
7" Dolphin Comporte

1950/23
3 Pc. Open Border Mayonnaise Set

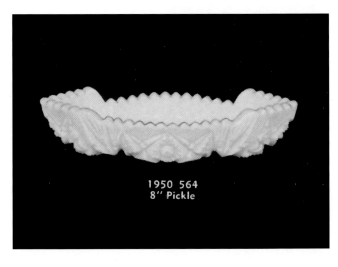

1950 564
8" Pickle

1950/156
4½" Breakfast Marmalade Jar
& Cover

1950/505, 1
Cruet & Stopper

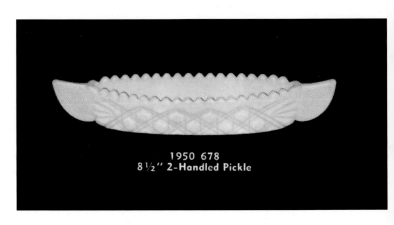

1950 678
8½" 2-Handled Pickle

Decanters and Sets

11/592 Tom and Jerry Set Decorated Gold, 11 pieces. $160-185.

Catalog Illustrations

11/592	Tom and Jerry Mug, Gold Decorated	1935,1943	$10-12
11/592	Tom and Jerry Bowl, Gold Decorated	1935,1943	$60-65
1950/500	15 Piece Punch Set (no picture)	1955-58	$*
1950/5	14 Piece Punch Set	1964-68	$200-225
1950/169	Decanter and Stopper	1959-65	$100-110

No. 5
14 Pc. Punch Set
(91 Crystal Ladle)

11/592
9-pc. Tom & Jerry Set
(gold decorated)

11/592
7-pc. Tom & Jerry Set
(gold decorated)

11/592
13-pc. Tom & Jerry Set
(gold decorated)

11/592
Tom & Jerry Mug (8)

11/592
Tom & Jerry Mug (6)

11/592
Tom & Jerry Mug (12)

1950 169
Decanter & Stopper

Salt and Pepper Sets, Cream and Sugar Sets

1950/4283 Miniature Basket with Salt and Pepper. $35-40 set.

1950/266 Snow Woman
Salz. $30-35.

1950/335 Owl Sugar and Cream Set. $35-40 set.

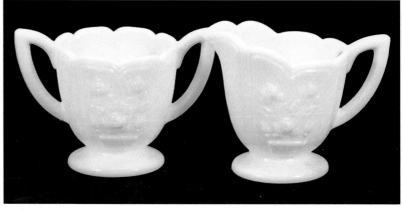

1950/588 Sugar and Cream Set. $18-22 set.

1950/304 Spoon Holder Sugar. $15-20.

1950/799 Sugar and Cream Set,
Ivy. $18-20 set.

Catalog Illustrations

1950/265	Snowman Pfeffer	1955-60	$30-35
1950/266	Snow Woman Salz	1955-60	$30-35
1950/267	Salz and Pfeffer	1955-60	$60-70
1950/300	3 Piece Caster Set	1951-55	$30-35
1950/617	Seasoning Shaker Jar and Cover	1963-66	$35-40
1950/31	3-Toed Sugar and Cream Set	1957-62	$25-30
1950/95	Sugar and Cream Set	1955-58	$25-30

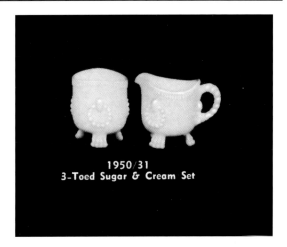

1950/31
3-Toed Sugar & Cream Set

1950/300 3 pc.
Caster Set

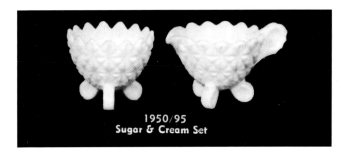

1950/95
Sugar & Cream Set

1950/267
Salz & Pfeffer Set

1950/617
Seasoning Shaker Jar
and Cover

1950/641/2	Salt and Pepper Glossy Only (51474)	1978-78	$18-20	
1950/4283	Miniature Basket with Salt & Pepper	1950-66	$35-40	
1950/42	Miniature Salt and Pepper Set	1950-66	$10-15	
1950/204	Jar and Cover, Dolphin, (Doeskin Only)	1955-55	$15-20	
1950/205	Sugar and Cream, Dolphin, (Doeskin Only)	1955-55	$30-40	
1950/206	Cream Pitcher, (Doeskin Only)	1955-55	$15-20	
1950/226	4-Toed Sugar (Part of 1950/228)	1955-60	$20-22	
1950/227	4-Toed Cream Pitcher (part of 1950/228)	1955-60	$20-22	
1950/228	4-Toed Sugar and Cream (both covered)	1955-60	$40-45	
1950/230	Oval Cream Pitcher (part of 1950/232)	1955-60	$20-25	
1950/231	Oval Sugar and Cream (part of 1950/232, no covers)	1955-60	$40-50	
1950/232	Oval Sugar and Cream, both covered	1955-60	$20-25	

1950/301	Cream Pitcher (in 1950/305 Set)	1953-60	$12-15
1950/304	Sugar and Cover (in 1950/305 Set)	1953-60	$15-20
1950/305	Spoon Holder Covered Sugar and Cream	1952-60	$35-40
1950/335	Owl Sugar and Cream	1955-60	$35-40
1950/528	Sugar and Cream, Flower	1955-58	$15-20
1950/588	Sugar and Cream Set	1955-68	$18-22
1950/595	Sugar and Cream Set	1955-58	$18-22
1950/598	Sugar and Cream Set	1955-58	$18-22
1950/698	Sugar and Cream Set, Monticello	1955-58	$18-22
1950/740	Sugar and Cream Set	1955-58	$18-20
1950/760	Sugar and Cream Set	1955-58	$18-20
1950/799	Sugar and Cream, Ivy	1955-58	$18-20

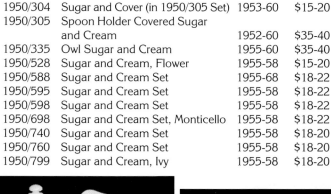

1950/305
Spoon Holder Sugar & Cream Set
Consists of:
1950/304 Sugar & Cover
1950/301 Cream Pitcher

1950/335
Owl Sugar & Cream Set

51474
Salt & Pepper Set

1950/641/2
Salt and Pepper Glossy Only
(51474)

1950/4283
Miniature Basket with Salt & Pepper

1950/528
Sugar & Cream Set

1950/588
Sugar & Cream Set

1950/595
Sugar & Cream Set

1950 598
Sugar & Cream Set

1950 698
Sugar & Cream Set

1952/204 Jar and Cover   1952/206 Cream Pitcher
1952/205 Sugar and Cream Set

1950/740
Sugar & Cream Set

1950/760
Sugar & Cream Set

1950 228
4-Toed Sugar & Cream Set

1950 232
Oval Sugar & Cream Set

1950/799
Sugar & Cream Set

Vases

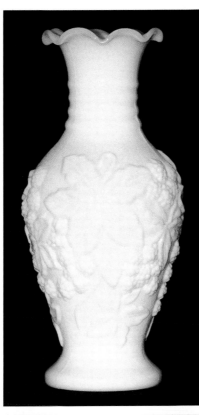

1950/178, 7 1/2"
Pinched Vase.
$15-17.

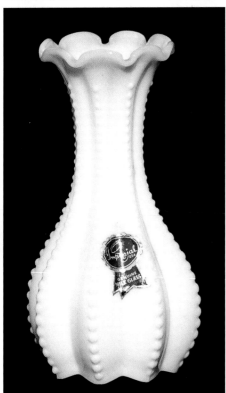

Top: 1950/22, 5" Vase, Pineapple.
$10-12.

Bottom: 1950/86, 5" Vase. This vase comes in many colors and makes a neat small collection. $10-12.

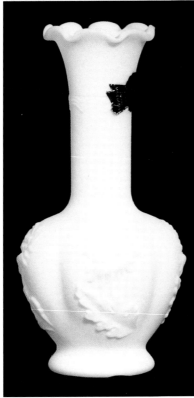

Top: 1950/109, 6" Vase, Loganberry. $12-15.

Bottom: 1950/111, 6" Vase, Mum. $12-15.

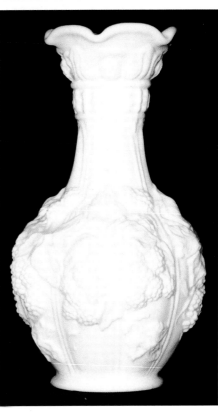

1950/356, 10" Crimped Vase, Loganberry. This was a very popular mold with Imperial and the vases can be found in many colors. Carnival colors include Peacock, Rubigold, Meadow Green, White, Horizon Blue, Pink, Amber, and Amethyst. This popular vase can also be found in Azure Blue, Ultra Blue, Nut Brown, Fern Green, Blue Satin, Ivory Satin, and Satin Crystal, as well as Milk Glass. $20-25 for milk glass vase.

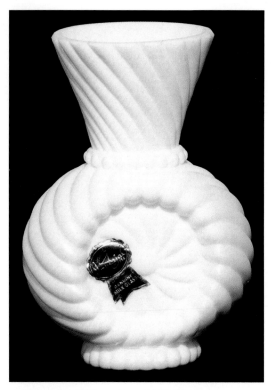

1950/457, 5" Vase, Spiral. $15-20.

1950/612, 11 1/2" Footed Whisk Broom Vase.
$25-30.

11/153, 8" Footed Bud
Vase. $20-22.

1950/613, 6" Bud
Vase, Whisk Broom.
$15-18.

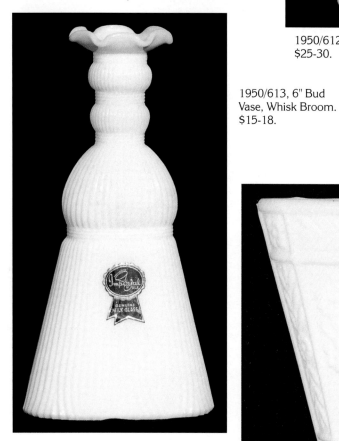

1950/605 Wall Pocket Vase. Finding this
vase was a thrill! It provided a picture for
the company identification number of
1950/605. $50-55.

1950/132, 8 1/4" Urn. The Doeskin
finish on this vase makes the design
outstanding. $50-55.

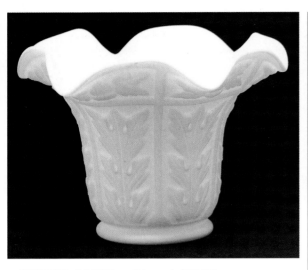

1950/663, 4 1/2" Vase Crimped. $15-20.

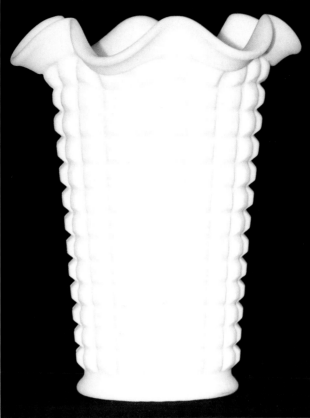

1950/699C, 6 1/2" Vase, Crimped, Monticello. Imperial used #699 as the line number for Washington. It is strange that here the item name is Monticello, which is the #698 line. Perhaps this was an error on the numbering of this item, but it will be left as Imperial numbered it. $18-20.

1950/981, 5" Pitcher Vase. $12-15.

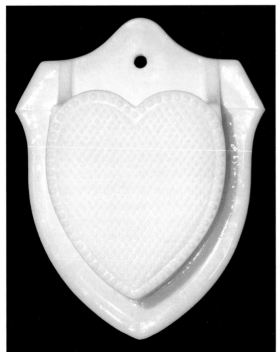

1950/143, 6 1/2" Love Bird Vase. $32-35.

1950/895 Heart Wall Pocket. This Heart Wall Pocket was an exciting new discovery! Several of them showed up in an Imperial worker's estate sale—the vase and identification number were an important addition to our information. The Heart Wall Pocket does not appear in a catalog or price list so the production date is unknown, but it was probably made in the 1950s. It is *not* marked. $*

Catalog Illustrations

1950/22	5" Vase, Pineapple	1950-68	$10-12
1950/28C	5" Whimsical Ivy, Pineapple	1950-69	$10-12
1950/33	6" Footed Vase	1950-52	$20-22
1950/76	6" Vase, Basket of Flowers	1956-60	$18-20
1950/86	5" Vase (51757)	1953-59, 1978-78	$10-12
1950/87	Miniature Fiddle Vase	1951-52	$20-25
1950/88	Miniature Banjo Vase	1951-52	$20-25
1950/89	Miniature Vase	1951-52	$18-20
1950/90	Miniature Vase	1951-52, 1954-58	$18-20
1950/93	2 Piece Epergne Set	1951-52	$30-40
1950/98	8" Vase, Toed	1959-62	$25-30
1950/109	6" Vase, Loganberry	1953-71	$12-15
1950/111	6" Vase, Mum	1953-69	$12-15
1950/112	6" Vase, Jonquil	1955-69	$18-20
1950/132	8 1/4" Urn, Dancing Nudes	1950-54	$50-55
1950/143	6 1/2" Love Bird Vase	1951-60	$32-35
11/153	8" Footed Bud Vase	1943	$20-22
1950/178	7 1/2" Pinched Vase	1958-60	$15-17
1950/184	8" TV Vase, One Side Sun Dial	1951-51	$30-35
1950/185	Blown Fiddle Vase	1951-55	$20-22
1950/186	Blown Banjo Vase	1951-55	$20-22
1950/194	9 1/4" Celery Vase	1952-60	$15-17
1950/189	7" Footed Ivy	1953-55	$20-25
1950/190	7" Footed Vase	1953-55	$20-25
1950/192	8 1/2" Tricorn Vase	1951-58	$20-22
1950/212	6" Vase (no picture)	1962-65	$*
1950/356	10" Crimp Vase, Loganberry (51774)	1950-79	$20-25
1950/457	5" Vase, Spiral	1957-62	$15-20
1950/466	5 1/4" Vase	1958-69	$12-15
1950/467	4 1/2" Ivy Jar (no picture)	1958-68	$*
1950/480	9 1/2" Vase	1956-62	$30-35
1950/486	8 1/2" Masque Vase (11/486C)	1943, 1952-58	$30-35
1950/488	12" Umbrella Vase (11/488)	1930s, 1943	$32-35
1950/488	12" Umbrella Vase (same as above) (51775)	1950-59, 1977-78	$32-35
1950/605	6" Wall Pocket Vase, V Shape (see photo, p. 140)	1959-60	$50-55
1950/610	7 1/4" Wall Vase, Whisk Broom	1960-60, 1964-68	$50-55
1950/612	11 1/2" Footed Whisk Broom Vase (see photo, p. 140)	1964-66	$25-30
1950/613	6" Bud Vase, Whisk Broom	1964-68	$15-18
1950/661	5 1/4" Vase	1956-64	$15-17
1950/662	4 1/2" Vase	1956-60	$12-17
1950/663	4 1/2" Vase, Crimp	1956-62	$15-20
1950/699	6 1/2" Vase, Monticello	1955-60	$18-20
1950/699C	6 1/2" Vase Crimped, Monticello	1956-60	$18-20
1950/895	Heart Wall Pocket (see photo, p. 141)		$*
1950/980	5" Pitcher Vase	1960-62	$12-15
1950/981	5" Pitcher Vase	1960-68	$12-15
1950/5016	Footed Wedding Vase (no picture)	1957-58	$*
11/775	10" Blown Vase	1930s, 1943	$20-25
1950/1186	4" Blown Vase (see photo, p. 85)	1959-59	$*

1950/22
5" Vase, Pineapple

1950/28C
5" Whimsical Ivy

1950/33
6" Footed Vase

1950/76
6" Vase

1950/86
5" Vase

1950/87
Miniature Fiddle Vase

1950 88
Miniature Banjo Vase

1950/89
Miniature Vase

1950 90
Miniature Vase

1950/93
2 pc. Epergne Set

1950 98
8" Vase, Toed

1950/109
6" Vase, Loganberry

1950/111
6" Vase, Mum

1950/112
6" Vase, Jonquil

1950/132
8¼" Urn

**1950/143
6½" Love Bird Vase**

11/153 8 in. Ftd.
Bud Vase

1950/178
7½" Pinched Vase

1950/184
8" TV Vase
(Reverse Side has sun-
dial decoration)

1950/185
Blown Fiddle Vase

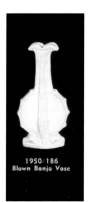

1950/186
Blown Banjo Vase

1950/194
9¼" Celery Vase

1950/189
7" Footed Ivy

1950 190
7" Footed Vase

1950/192
8½" Tricorn Vase

1950/356
10" Crimped Vase, Loganberry

1950/457
5" Vase

1950 466
5¼" Vase

1950/480
9½" Vase

1950/486
8½" Masque Vase

1950 488
12" Umbrella Vase

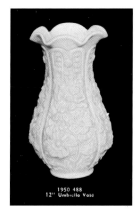

1950 610
7¼" Wall Vine
Vase

1950/613
6" Bud Vase

1950/661
5¼" Vase

1950/662
4½" Vase

1950/663
4½" Vase, Crimped

1950/699
6½" Vase

1950/699C
6½" Vase, Crimped

1950 980
5" Pitcher Vase

1950 981
5" Pitcher Vase

11/775 10 in. Blown Vase

143

Miscellaneous

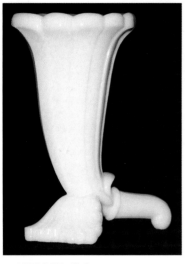

1950/107, 6" Cornucopia
$15-17.

1950/340 Colonial Hat. $30-35.

1950/282 Americana Jar and Cover. $40-45.

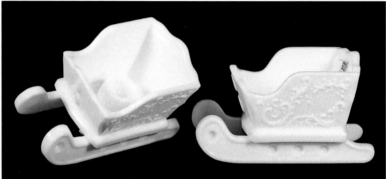

1950/346 Sleigh 6" Long. The company records only indicate one small sleigh. However, there are two: our sleigh (shown on the right) is plain on the inside, while one owned by a friend (shown on the left) features a candleholder in the sleigh compartment. Both would have been made with the same mold, but by using a different plunger the candleholder was formed. Both are marked with the IG. $*

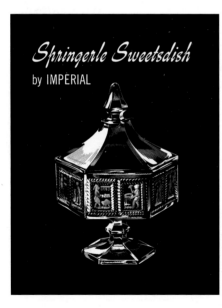

Springerle Sweetsdish
by IMPERIAL

Springerle Sweetsdish with the storybook POPA Tag. Inside reads: "This beautiful Springerle Sweetsdish has *never before* appeared on the market anywhere in the world! Genuinely new and as genuinely original, it was inspired by a Wooden Cookie Roller and a metal reproduction of a still existing German Springerle Cookie Mould used over 300 years ago. Design and Function are pleasantly wed in this Decorative Server. It will enhance the 'personality' of your home! Deliberately designed for and at first only produced in water-clear, quality Crystal, it is now (by popular demand) also available in several Colors." The Springerle box and cover was also made in milk glass from 1964-66. $30-35.

Below left: 1950/376 Wheelbarrow 11 3/4" (3 1/8 pounds!) Note the raised vertical panels on the sides. Rare. $*

Below right: 1950/??? Wheelbarrow. A wheelbarrow with a missing leg was offered for sale during the work on this book. Knowing of our project, a friend bought it for us. Wonderful! It is unlikely that Imperial made two pieces so much alike. It is possible, however, that they first designed and made the plain wheelbarrow, then decided to chip the vertical panels into the mold. Was the plain wheelbarrow ever put on the market? Only time will tell, if and when other plain ones surface. Both wheelbarrows have the IG mark on the bottom. $*

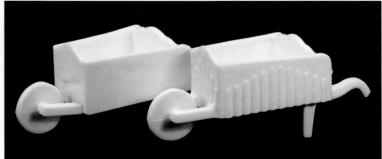

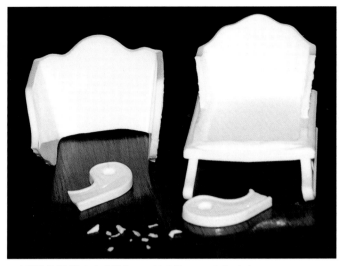

1950/347 Sleigh 11" Long (4 1/4 pounds!). At last we were going to have a sleigh to photograph so collectors would know how this coveted item looks. A very special friend packed this with great care but look how it arrived! When we photographed the damaged sleigh, we did not expect to include it in the book. After the initial shock, however, it gave us a chuckle to think about showing it in this condition. This sleigh, too, has the IG mark. Rare $*

1950/347 Sleigh 11" Long. The repaired sleigh makes a wonderful shelf piece! Notice that the holes on the runner of this sleigh are not open—they are indented, but closed. A factory photo shows the sleigh with open holes. We wonder which was first: the open holes or the indentations? $*

1950/910 Whisk Broom Box. *Imperial Glass Photograph.* $20-25.

1950/377 Pie Wagon. *Imperial Glass Photograph.* $200-225.

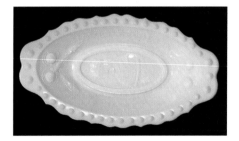

1950/213 (51599), 9" Pickle "Loves Request." $20-30.

1950/88 Miniature Banjo Vase, 1950/101 Miniature Boot, 1950/89 Miniature Vase, and 1950/90 Miniature Vase. The boot is the most common of this group; the others are seldom seen. They range in height from 2 3/4" to 3 1/2". Prices vary. $12-25 each.

1950/809 Colonial Belle. $35-40.

Catalog Illustrations

1950/59	5 1/2" Jar and Cover, Peanut, Mint or Butter	1952-60	$20-25
1950/101	Miniature Boot (11/100)	1943, 1950-51	$12-15
1950/102	Miniature Urn (11/102)	1943, 1950-52	$12-15
11/103	Miniature Pitcher (no vertical lines)	1943	$12-15
1950/104	Miniature Pitcher, (vertical lines)	1951-52	$12-15
1950/106	Miniature Pitcher (design on outside)	1952-52	$12-15
11/106	Miniature Pitcher (no design on outside) (no picture)	1930s	$12-15
1950/107	6" Cornucopia	1952-55	$15-17

1950/144	5" Covered Puff, Pin or Desk Box	1950-52	$35-40
1950/176	4 Toed-Jar and Cover	1960-64	$30-35
1950/210	Peanut and Shaving Mug, Robin	1953-55	$15-17
1950/213	9" Pickle "Loves Request" (51599)	1978-78	$20-30
1950/282	Americana Jar	1956-62	$40-45
1950/340	Colonial Hat	1955-58	$30-35
1950/618	Springerle Box & Cover (no picture)	1964-66	$30-35

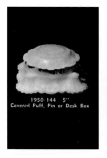

1950-144 5"
Covered Puff, Pin or Desk Box

1950 176
4 Toed Jar & Cover

1950 210
Shaving Mug, Ivy, or Peanut Jar

1950.59
5½" Jar & Cover,
(Peanut, Mint, or Butter)

11/100 Boot

11/102 Urn

51599
9" Pickle Dish

11/103 Pitcher

1950/104
Miniature Pitcher

1950/106
Miniature Pitcher

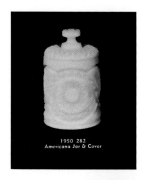

1950 282
Americana Jar & Cover

1950/107
6" Cornucopia

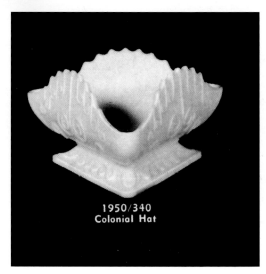

1950/340
Colonial Hat

1950/303	Carving Knife Rest	1950-62	$45-50
1950/346	Little Sleigh, 6" Long (see photo, p. 144)	?-?	$*
1950/???	Little Sleigh With Candleholder, 6" Long (see photo, p. 144)	?-?	$*
1950/347	Sleigh 11" Long (see photo, p. 145)	1958-59	$*
1950/376	Wheelbarrow 11 3/4" (see photo, p. 144)	1958-60	$*
1950/377	Pie Wagon and Cover (see photo, p. 145)	1959-60	$200-225
1950/385	6 3/4" Horseshoe Ash Tray	1956-58	$15-17
1950/666	5 1/2" Handled Box (no picture)	1958-60	$*
1950/906	6 Piece Miniature Lamb Set	1959-60	$100-125
1950/736	"Butterpat" Box and Cover (41870)	1964-69, 1977-78	$20-22
1950/809	7 1/2" Colonial Belle Box	1966-68	$50-55
1950/809	Colonial Belle (51844)	1955-58, 1977-78	$35-40
1950/910	7" Whisk Broom Box (see photo, p. 145)	1959-60	$20-25
1591	Story Book Mug (51320)	1978-78	$40-45

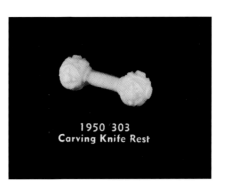

1950 303
Carving Knife Rest

1950/385
6 3/4" Horseshoe Ash Tray

1950/906
6 Piece Miniature Lamb Set

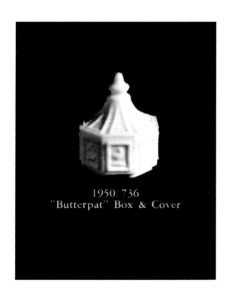

1950/736
"Butterpat" Box & Cover

1950/809
Colonial Belle

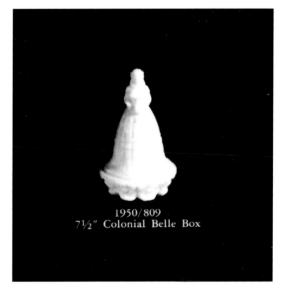

1950/809
7 1/2" Colonial Belle Box

51320
Storybook Mug

11/106 and 1950/104 Miniature Pitchers. Shown here is the 11/106 early version that has no design on it. There is a later version (1950/106, not shown) that has vertical ribs and flowers on it. The early version of 11/103 (not shown) has no vertical ribs but does have a band of squares around it. Shown here is the later version of the (11/103) 1950/104 with the vertical ribs and squares circling it. These are examples of some of the unusual numbering that Imperial used. Considering the vast numbers of items produced by Imperial, however, the confusing numbers were very minute. $20-25 each.

Certificate of Authenticity. Certificates were placed in each of the limited edition Cambridge Dresden Dolls. These 346 items were produced on June 26, 1981, the last day Imperial used the LIG hallmark.

CERTIFICATE OF AUTHENTICITY

June 26, 1981 was the last day Imperial produced items with the ⊡ hallmark. On this day we produced the limited edition Cambridge Dresden Doll in a quantity of only 346 pieces. Thank you for your continued interest in Imperial Glass.

Lucile J. Kennedy
Lucile J. Kennedy
Imperial Glass Corporation

This photo (2 1/2' by 3') hung on Imperial's factory wall from the 1950s until the company's closing in 1984. This is one of several photos that proudly displayed the lines for which Imperial was known: Milk Glass, Cape Cod, Candlewick, and Washington to name a few. These photos are now in private homes, along with collections of the patterns captured in the photos.

Imperial Glass Corporation
advertisements, c. 1950.

149

Closing Thoughts

We are at the point where this needs to come to a close. Already we have gone into many more avenues than we planned in the beginning—there never seems to be a stopping place! We know that every detail may not be complete, and that more or different information may come to light. As stated in our book *Imperial Cape Cod: Tradition to Treasure* ©1991, "We have taken a risk in publishing this book, and we have left ourselves open to close scrutiny, so please be gentle. Until you have undertaken a task such as this, you have no idea how perfect you are expected to be and, we are not perfect." We hope you will enjoy this book as much as we will enjoy it, once it is finished!

Consider the old adage: "It is a strong marriage that survives building a home." We survived that once, even survived an extensive addition to our home. One might also test the strength of a marriage following retirement. But, if you really want to test a marriage, try researching and writing a book together. Having been through all of this, we have decided we are survivors.

1950/505 Cigarette or Toothpick Holder. What an interesting collection one can build from such a small item. Several of the colors shown here were also made in satin finishes. Imperial was famous for producing many items in many different colors.

Chards from the Imperial factory site. These are among the pieces that we picked up just a week before the factory was leveled. Note the milk glass piece with the "flutes" that was the stopper to a cologne. It took us several years to find a milk glass set using this stopper.

Imperial Glass advertisements, c. 1950.

151

Endnotes

[1]Author unknown, "Story of Hand-Made Milk Glass," Bellaire, Ohio, Imperial Glass Corporation,1951.

[2]Imperial Glass Corporation Factory Note, January 1, 1950.

[3]Imperial Glass Corporation Factory Note, January 1, 1950.

[4]Inside Back Cover, Imperial Glass Corporation Catalog B, 1952.

[5]Author unknown, "Story of Hand-Made Milk Glass," Bellaire, Ohio, Imperial Glass Corporation,1951.

[6]Imperial Glass Corporation Factory Note, January 1, 1950.

[7]Inside Back Cover, Imperial Glass Corporation Catalog B, 1952.

[8]Author unknown, "Story of Hand-Made Milk Glass," Bellaire, Ohio, Imperial Glass Corporation,1951.

[9]Imperial Belknap Folder, 1955.

[10]Imperial Tag for Atterbury Items, 1957.

[11]Imperial Glass Corporation Factory Note, January 1, 1950.

[12]Imperial Advertising Brochure, 1958.

[13]Imperial Glass Corporation, Facts From The House of Americana Glass, 1959.

[14]Imperial Glass Corporation, Factory Paper - Questions and Answers, Undated.

[15]Imperial Genuine Purple Slag Glass Tie Tag, Undated.

[16]Imperial Glass Corporation Factory-Questions and Answers, Undated.

[17]Imperial Catalog, 1977.

[18]Author unknown, Certificate of Authenticity Metropolitan Museum of Art, 1976.

Appendix I
Where the Molds Are

Due to the liquidation of Imperial Glass Corporation, the company's molds were sold to many different companies and individuals. Below is an attempt to provide collectors with a list showing where the molds are that were used to produce milk glass items through the years. Although this list may not be complete, we feel very fortunate to be able to include this information. A big "thank you" goes to Helen Clark for helping with this section.

Bellaire Glass Festival

/102

Boyd Glass

/19	/60	/73	/76	/81	/201
/218	/225	/346	/459	/500	/720
/736	/750	/906	/1776	/271-273	

Fenton

/230	/231	/241	/285	/310	/329
/458	/488	/598	/743	/779	/859

Maroon Enterprises

/120	/125	/220	/347	/376	/790

Mirror Images

/87	/88	/89	/90	/300

Pairpoint Glass

/109

Save Imperial Group

/31	/236	/799	/801

Silver Dollar Trading

/38	/59	/112	/115	/116	/131
/134	/140	/163	/206	/234	/244
/270	/321	/322	/356	/473 sherbet	
/615	/630 juice	/630 sherbet	/662	/760	
/473 goblet					

L.E. Smith

/13	/29	/30	/40	/45	/47
/49	/52	/54	/58	/62	/65
/67	/72	/74	/80	/111	/113
/133	/156	/160	/188	/189	/19 ivy
/191 jewel box	/192	/194	/199	/204	/225
/239	/240	/259	/260	/265	/292
/293	/295	/303	/385	/450	/456
/461	/464	/466	/514	/520	/610
/743	/778	/880			

Summit Art Glass

/24	/25	/26	/155	/161	/170
/306	/335	/495	/624	/630	/800

R. Wetzel Glass

/435	/528	/772	/682

Rastal Gmbh & Co. K.G.

/55	/56	/73	/85	/103	/110
/192	/217	/296	/336	375/	/422
/433	/463	/465	/473 pt. Pit.	/514	/618
/638	/640	/641	/642	/730	/735
/780	/815	/817	/818	/840	/858

Indiana Glass

/62	/90	108	/109	/145	/146
/148	/185	/186	/356		

Tiara Exclusives

/147	/149	/157	/158	/159	/214
/294	/312	/377	/400	/462	/809
/860	/974	/975			

Price Guide by Mold Number

This price list for Imperial milk glass has been compiled by using prices seen on pieces for sale in antique malls, shops, and shows in various states. Several collectors contributed information used for this list. An asterisk (*) has been used when there was too little information to conclusively determine an item's price.

Items that are sought by different groups of collectors will always command higher prices because of the competition to obtain certain pieces. In addition, the hand decorated, metal combinations, and other specialty items usually command prices that are relatively higher as well. Until collectors learn about the vast selection of Imperial milk glass and opaque glass, prices will fluctuate greatly. Prices ultimately will stabilize at the amount the collector is willing to pay.

This list is to be used as a guideline only—the authors assume no responsibility for any of the pricing information herein. As noted earlier, remember that "prices are in the eyes of the beholder" and "judge a price by demand, desirability, and the length of time an item was produced."

Mold No.	Description	Dates	Price
1950/1D	6 1/2" Plate, Grape	1954-68	$5-7
1950/3D	7 1/2" Plate, Grape	1954-69	$5-7
1950/5	14 Piece Punch Set	1964-68	$200-225
1950/5D	8 1/2" Plate, Grape	1954-66	$8-10
1950/5D	8" Plate, Salad or Wall, Open Border	1950-50	$8-10
1950/6C	8" Crimped Bowl, Grape	1954-71	$10-12
1950/6D	9 1/2" Wall or Luncheon Plate, Grape	1954-71	$10-12
1950/7D	9" Plate Wall or Luncheon, Windmill	1950-60	$15-20
1950/9	Bundling Lamp, (Glossy Only)	1954-65	$90-100
1950/10D	10 1/2" Wall or Buffet Plate, Rose	1950-71	$15-20
1950/13D	12 1/2" Torte or Wall Plate, Rose	1950-64	$20-22
1950/20	14 Piece Wassail Set, Grape	1950-50	*
1950/21	6" Vase, Grape	1930s,1943, 1950-50	$15-17
1950/22	5" Vase Pineapple	1950-68	$10-12
1950/23	3 Piece Mayonnaise, Open Border	1950-50	$20-22
1950/23B	5 1/2" Dessert Bowl, Open Border	1950-50	$6-8
1950/23D	7 1/2" Bread and Butter, Open Border	1950-50	$6-8
1950/24	3 Pint Water Pitcher, Rose	1950-50	$35-40
1950/25	Covered Sugar, Rose	1950-60	$15-20
1950/26	Cream Pitcher, Rose	1950-60	$15-20
1950/28C	5" Whimsical Ivy, Pineapple	1950-69	$10-12
1950/29	5" Fish Ash Tray	1952-52	$20-22
1950/30	Sugar and Cream, Lace Edge	1950-50, 1955-60	$20-25
1950/31	3-Toed Sugar and Cream	1957-62	$25-30
1950/32	5" Fruit, Grape, Pear Shape (in 1950/8532 Set)	1952-60	$6-8
1950/33	6" Footed Vase	1950-52	$20-22
1950/38	6 oz. Pitcher, Grape (in 1950/3839 Set)	1954-65	$15-17
1950/39	Saucer, Grape, (in 1950/3839 Set)	1954-65	$8-10
1950/40	9 1/2" Basket, Daisy	1950-64	$30-35
1950/42	Miniature Salt and Pepper	1950-66	$10-15
1950/45	5" Jelly Compote, "Candlewick" (Lines and Flower Center)	1950-60	$35-40
1950/45	5" Jelly Compote, "Candlewick" (No Lines and Plain Center)	?-?	$35-40
1950/47	8" Berry Bowl, Grape	1952-71	$20-22
1950/47C	9" Crimped Bowl, Grape	1954-71	$20-22
1950/48	7" Centre Comporte	1950-52	$22-25
1950/49	4 1/2" Berry Bowl, Grape (51552)	1952-67, 1978-78	$8-10
1950/52C	8" Crimped Bowl, Windmill	1950-60	$20-22
1950/54	8" Relish, Horseshoe	1956-60	$15-20
1950/55	9" Partitioned Relish, Apple	1951-52	$20-22
1950/56	12" Partitioned Relish, Pear Shape	1951-52	$25-30
1950/58A	8" Oval Bowl, Windmill	1952-55	$18-20
1950/58C	9" Crimp Plate, Windmill	1952-55	$18-20
1950/58D	9 1/2" Oval Plate, Windmill	1952-55	$20-22
1950/59	5 1/2" Jar and Cover	1952-60	$20-25
1950/60	5 1/2" Honey or Peanut Jar (11/60)	1943, 1950-60	$50-55
1950/62C	9" Crimped Bowl, Rose (51699)	1950-71, 1977-78	$20-22
1950/65	Oblong Candy Box and Cover	1955-58	$35-40
1950/66C	5 1/2" Crimped Bon Bon Hobnail (51720)	1950-71, 1977-78	$18-20
1950/67	8 1/2" Fruit Compote, Vinelf	1950-65	$35-40
1950/68D	10 1/2" Pastry Tray	1950-50	$20-22
1950/69	6" Square Bowl	1952-60	$15-17
1950/70	6 oz. Oil or Vinegar, Washington	1950-50	$30-35
1950/72	12 x 9 1/2" Salad or Dessert Bowl, Pear Shape	1951-52	$25-30
1950/73	5" Pansy Basket	1952-69	$20-25
1950/74	3-Toed Bowl, Rose (51670)	1952-59, 1977-78	$22-25
1950/75C	11" Crimped Fruit Bowl, "Candlewick"	1950-52	$60-65
1950/75D	11" Buffet or Wall Plate, "Candlewick"	1950-52	$60-65
1950/75F	11" Coupe Apple Bowl, "Candlewick"	1950-51	$60-65
1950/75H	9" Heart Fruit or Dessert Bowl, "Candlewick"	1950-52	$100-125
1950/76	6" Vase, Basket Of Flowers	1956-60	$18-20
1950/78	9 1/2" Footed Jar, Lace Edge	1962-62	$20-25
1950/78C	6" Candleholder, Lace Edge	1956-60	$10-12
1950/79	2 Piece Hurricane, 11 1/2",		

Item	Description	Years	Price
	Crystal Shade	1950-50	$40-50
1950/80	7 1/2" Vinelf Candleholder	1950-65	$25-30
1950/81	5" Handled Candleholder	1952-59	$10-12
1950/81	5" Footed and Handled Candleholder	1964-69	$12-15
1950/85	14" Oblong Tray	1952-60	$22-25
1950/86	5" Vase (51757)	1953-59, 1978-78	$10-12
1950/87	Miniature Fiddle Vase	1951-52	$20-25
1950/88	Miniature Banjo Vase	1951-52	$20-25
1950/89	Miniature Vase	1951-52	$18-20
1950/90	Miniature Vase	1951-52, 1954-58	$18-20
1950/90	8" Dolphin Candleholder (51792)	1954-58, 1977-78	$20-25
1950/92	9 1/2" 3-Toed Bowl	1951-52	$25-28
1950/93	2 Piece Epergne	1951-52	$30-40
1950/94	4 1/2" x 5" Candy, Covered and Handled, Cape Cod	1952-55	$65-75
1950/95	Sugar and Cream	1955-58	$25-30
1950/96	Salt and Pepper, Grape (51484)	1954-70, 1978-78	$15-20
1950/96	Salt and Pepper, Hobnail (Glossy Only) (51480)	1977-78	$15-20
1950/98	8" Vase Toed	1959-62	$25-30
1950/100	4" Twin Candleholder	1950-68	$8-10
1950/101	Miniature Boot (11/100)	1943, 1950-51	$12-15
1950/102	Miniature Urn (11/102)	1943, 1950-52	$12-15
1950/103	10" Footed Fruit Bowl, "Candlewick"	1950-60	$60-70
1950/104	Miniature Pitcher (11/103)	1943, 1951-52	$12-15
1950/106	Miniature Pitcher (Design on Outside)	1952-52	$12-15
1950/106	Miniature Pitcher (No Design Outside)	1930s	$12-15
1950/107	6" Cornucopia	1952-55	$15-17
1950/108	6" Vase, Rose (51751)	1953-70, 1978-78	$15-17
1950/109	6" Vase, Loganberry	1953-71	$12-15
1950/110	10 1/2" 1-lb. Covered Candy	1950-55	$15-20
1950/111	6" Vase, Mum	1953-69	$12-15
1950/112	6" Vase, Jonquil	1955-69	$18-20
1950/113C	11 1/2" 3-Toed Crimped Fruit, Rose	1950-69	$30-35
1950/114	7 1/4" Lamp Vase, Lipped Crimp, Grape	1955-60	$25-27
1950/114	7 1/4" Lamp Vase, Hobnail (Glossy Only) (51762)	1977-78	$27-30
1950/115	10 3/4" Footed Lamp Vase, Grape	1956-60	$40-45
1950/116	6" Vase, Rose	1956-60	$15-18
1950/119	9 1/2" Crucifix Candleholder (11/119)	1943, 1955-55	$80-85
1950/120	Bridesmaid Bowl and Cover, Scroll	1952-62	$25-27
1950/120C	5 1/2" Footed Crimped Bowl, Scroll	1958-62	$20-25
1950/123	Toast and Clear Cover, Cupped, Grape Plate (Clear Cover)	1954-55	$95-110
1950/125	Wedding Bowl and Cover, Scroll	1953-61	$35-40
1950/128	15 Piece Punch, Grape (11/473)	1943, 1952-65	$175-185
1950/128	Bowl Base, Grape (11/473)	1943, 1952-65,	$30-35
1950/128	Bowl Only (11/473)	1943, 1950-65	$40-45
1950/131	Festive Bowl and Cover	1952-55	$30-32
1950/131B	7 1/4" x 7 1/4" Footed Bowl	1952-55	$20-22
1950/132	8 1/4" Urn Dancing Nudes	1950-54	$50-55
1950/133	1-lb. Footed Candy and Cover	1950-52	$30-35
1950/134	Hobby Horse Cigarette Box	1950-50	*
1950/137	Double Candleholder, Grape	1959-61	$30-35
1950/140	Candy Jar and Cover, Pineapple	1951-52	$40-45
1950/143	6 1/2" Lovebird Vase	1951-60	$32-35
1950/144	5" Covered Puff, Pin, Desk Box	1950-52	$35-40
1950/145	4 1/2" Hen-On-Nest (11/145)	1930s, 1943	$25-30
1950/145	4 1/2" Hen-On-Nest (51926)	1950-71, 1977-78	$25-30
1950/146	4 1/2" Duck-On-Nest	1952-60	$30-35
1950/147	4" Swan Mint Whimsy (11/147)	1943, 1950-71	$20-25
1950/148	4 1/2" Swan-On-Nest	1951-60	$30-35
1950/149	5 1/2" Turkey-On-Nest	1952-60	$35-40
1950/150	4 1/2" Boudoir, or Desk Ash Tray	1950-52	$15-20
1950/152	Lamp Vase, (For Colonial Iron)	1957-61	$30-35
1950/154	Bird Box and Cover	1959-59	*
1950/155	Rabbit-On-Nest	1953-58	$200-225
1950/156	4 1/2" Breakfast Marmalade and Cover (11/54)	1930s, 1952-64	$18-20
1950/156	5 1/2" Basket	1968-71	$18-20
1950/157	"Rabbit" Box and Cover	1957-60	$250-300
1950/158	"Rooster" Box and Cover	1957-69	$175-200
1950/159	Atterbury Lion and Cover	1959-60	$225-250
1950/159/1	7 3/4" Atterbury Bowl	1959-69	$45-50
1950/160	3 1/2" Candleholder, Rose	1955-71	$10-12
1950/161	8" Covered Butter or Cheese, Rose	1950-64	$35-38
1950/162	Bunny-On-Nest (11/162)	1943, 1950-70	$25-30
1950/162	Bunny-On-Nest (51923)	1977-78	$25-30
1950/163	Decanter, Grape (11/473)	1943, 1950-68	$45-50
1950/164	9 oz. Lunch Goblet, "Leaf"	1950-50	$15-20
1950/164	6 oz. Lunch Sherbet, "Leaf"	1950-50	$15-20
1950/167	Duster or Shaker, Grape	1954-62	$15-20
1950/169	Decanter and Stopper	1959-65	$100-110
1950/170	Low Candleholder, "Candlewick"	1950-60	$20-25
1950/176	4-Toed Jar and Cover	1960-64	$30-35
1950/178	7 1/2" Pinch Vase	1958-60	$15-17
1950/179	8" Vase, Grape	1959-62	$25-30
1950/180	7 1/2" Vase, Grape	1955-68	$18-20
1950/181	6 1/4" Vase, Rose	1955-68	$22-25
1950/182	Vase, (For Colonial Iron)	1957-61	$30-35
1950/184	8" TV Vase, Reverse Side Sun-Dial	1951-51	$30-35
1950/185	Blown Fiddle Vase	1951-55	$20-22
1950/186	Blown Banjo Vase	1951-55	$20-22
1950/188	6 1/2" Footed Ivy, Hobnail (11/742N)	1943, 1950-64	$25-27
1950/188C	5" Crimp Compote, Hobnail (Glossy Only) (51720)	1978-78	$25-27
1950/189	7" Footed Ivy	1953-55	$20-25
1950/190	7" Footed Vase (Basket)	1953-55	$20-25
1950/191	Concord Ivy, Grape	1954-68	$18-20
1950/191	8 1/2" Partition Cigarette or Boudoir Box	1950-52	$80-85
1950/192	8 1/2" Tricorn Vase	1951-58	$20-22
1950/193	3 1/2" x 4" Jar, Cover, Handled Cape Cod	1952-53	$85-95
1950/194	9 1/4" Celery Vase	1952-60	$15-17
1950/196	2 Piece Epergne, "Candlewick" (Plain Vase, Center Flower)	?-?	$80-100
1950/196	2 Piece Epergne, "Candlewick" (Beaded Vase, No Center Flower)	1950-60	$80-100
1950/199	8" Shell Float, Candy or Relish	1950-52	$12-15
1950/200	5" Mug or Ivy, Cape Cod	1950-55	$60-65
1950/201	Cigarette Server, Grape	1950-69	$15-20
1950/201	14" Lamp, Peacock Feather	1962-62	$80-85
1950/201H	12" Handled Lamp	1962-62	$80-85
1950/203D	10" Cake Stand	1955-60	$25-30
1950/203F	8 1/4" Fruit Bowl	1955-64	$25-30
1950/204	Jar and Cover Dolphin (Doeskin Only)	1955-55	$15-20
1950/205	Sugar and Cream Dolphin (Doeskin Only)	1955-55	$30-40
1950/206	Cream Pitcher (Doeskin Only)	1955-55	$15-20
1950/207C	7 1/2" Bowl, Lace Edge (11/7455F)	1930s, 1953-65	$8-10
1950/207F	8" Bowl, Lace Edge (11/7566)	1930s, 1953-65	$8-10
1950/207K	5" Flower Arranger, Lace Edge	1965-69	$15-20

Item	Description	Years	Price
1950/207K	5" Bowl	1965-69	$8-10
1950/209	Cologne Bottle, Scroll	1956-58	$35-40
1950/210	Peanut or Shaving Mug, Robin	1953-55	$15-17
1950/212	6" Vase (No Picture)	1962-65	*
1950/213	9" Pickle, "Loves Request (51599)	1978-78	$20-30
1950/214	Atterbury Dove Box	1957-60	$175-200
1950/215	3 Partitioned Relish, Lace Edge	1955-55	$25-30
1950/216	Footed Salt and Pepper, Grape	1956-71	$18-20
1950/216	7 3/4" Boutique Lamp, Grape	1962-67	$50-55
1950/217	Hawaiian Server 5 1/2" x 11", Pineapple	1950-52	$22-25
1950/220C	10" Footed Crimp Bowl, Lace Edge	1957-60	$20-25
1950/220D	12" Footed Cake Stand, Lace Edge	1950-71	$25-30
1950/220E	12" Footed Banana Stand, Lace Edge	1950-68	$30-35
1950/220F	10" Footed Fruit Bowl, Lace Edge	1950-71	$25-30
1950/220X	9 1/2" Footed Bowl, Lace Edge	1951-52	$15-20
1950/221	8" Oval Daisy Button Basket	1955-60	$25-30
1950/225	Egg Cup, Grape	1954-62	$15-17
1950/226	4-Toed Sugar (Part of 1950/228 Set)	1955-60	$20-22
1950/227	4-Toed Cream Pitcher (Part of 1950/228 Set)	1955-60	$20-22
1950/228	4-Toed Sugar and Cream Both Covered	1955-60	$40-45
1950/230	Oval Cream Pitcher (Part of 1950/232 Set)	1955-60	$20-25
1950/231	Oval Sugar (Part of 1950/232 Set)	1955-60	$40-50
1950/232	Oval Sugar and Cream Both Covered	1955-60	$20-25
1950/234	Handled Cigarette Box, Grape	1957-60	$15-20
1950/234/3	3 Piece Cigarette, Grape (No Picture)	1957-60	*
1950/235	8" Berry Bowl, Scroll	1955-60	$15-20
1950/236	5" Nappy, Scroll	1955-60	$10-12
1950/236/1	Candleholder, Scroll	1958-60	$15-20
1950/239	Pitcher 3 Pint, Windmill (Shown in Set)	1950-52	$45-50
1950/240	Pitcher 1 Pint, Windmill	1950-65	$30-35
1950/241	Oil, Vinegar and Stopper, Grape	1953-65	$20-25
1950/244	Handled Box and Cover, Grape	1957-65	$17-20
1950/244C	5" Handled Nappy Crimp, Grape	1959-69	$12-15
1950/247	Salt and Pepper, Grape	1951-71	$18-20
1950/249	9 Piece Water Set, Rose	1950-50	$115-140
1950/252	13 1/2" Handled Basket	1951-55	$25-27
1950/255	7 1/2" 3 Partitioned Relish, Grape	1959-64	$40-45
1950/259	Candy Box and Cover	1952-60	$22-25
1950/260	"Watch" Candy Box and Cover	1958-60	$65-70
1950/265	Snowman Pfeffer	1955-60	$30-35
1950/266	Snow Woman Salz	1955-60	$30-35
1950/267	Salz and Pfeffer Set	1955-60	$60-70
1950/269	9 Piece Water Set, Windmill	1950-52	$125-135
1950/270	Candy Jar and Cover, Hobnail (51876)	1957-65, 1977-78	$25-30
1950/271	5" Heart, Lace Edge	1959-62	$20-25
1950/272	6" Heart, Lace Edge	1959-62	$20-25
1950/273	7" Heart, Lace Edge	1959-62	$20-25
1950/274C	7" 4-Toed Compote, Lace Edge	1953-65	$15-20
1950/275D	12" Snack Plate (No Picture)	1953-55	*
1950/275F	10" Bowl, Lace Edge	1953-66	$17-20
1950/276	1/4 Lb. Butter, Grape	1954-71	$30-35
1950/279	Twin Candleholder	1953-64	$10-12
1950/280	4" Candleholder	1950-50	$15-20
1950/282	Americana Jar and Cover	1956-62	$40-45
1950/285	Single Candleholder, Hobnail	1956-60	$10-12
1950/286B	5" Vase 4-Toed Lace Edge (11/743B)	1930s, 1953-62	$20-22
1950/287	10" Vase, Grape (9" 11/4731C)	1943, 1953-65	$25-30
1950/291	Atlantis (Shell) Ash Tray, Nut or Candy	1950-66	$10-12
1950/292	6 1/4" Double-Hand Ash Tray or Candy	1951-52	$30-35
1950/293	4 1/4" "Leaf" Ash Tray, Grape (51850)	1951-69, 1977-78	$6-8
1950/294	4 1/4" Heart Ash Tray	1951-55	$12-15
1950/295	6" Acorn Ash Tray	1951-52	$25-30
1950/296	10 1/2" Tray, Grape	1951-52	$35-40
1950/297	7 1/2" Shell Tray	1951-58	$12-15
1950/300	3 Piece Caster Set	1951-55	$30-35
1950/301	Cream Pitcher (in 1950/305 Set)	1953-60	$12-15
1950/303	Carving Knife Rest	1950-62	$45-50
1950/304	Sugar and Cover (in 1950/305 Set)	1953-60	$15-20
1950/305	Spoon Holder Covered Sugar and Cream	1952-60	$35-40
1950/306	1 qt. Pitcher, Grape	1955-62	$40-45
1950/307	6 oz. Footed Tumbler, Grape	1955-62	$8-10
1950/310	6" Bud Vase, Grape	1954-62	$12-15
1950/310	1-lb. Shenadoah Apple Candy Jar and Cover (No Picture)	1951-51	*
1950/311	1-lb. Pear Candy Jar and Cover, Beaded Block (No Picture)	1951-52	*
1950/311	Pitcher, Beaded Block, (No Picture)	1951-52	*
1950/311	Bud Vase, Beaded Block, (No Picture)	1951-52	*
1950/312	6" Candy Box and Cover, Heart Shape	1951-52	$25-30
1950/321	60 oz. Pitcher, Scroll	1955-60	$45-50
1950/322	11 oz. Goblet, Scroll	1956-60	$10-12
1950/322	7 oz. Sherbet, Scroll	1956-60	$10-12
1950/322	6 oz. Juice, Scroll	1956-60	$10-12
1950/322	5 oz. Wine, Scroll	1956-60	$10-12
1950/322	10 oz. Tumbler, Scroll	1956-60	$10-12
1950/322	12 oz. Ice Tea, Scroll	1955-60	$10-12
1950/325	3 1/4" Candleholder	1955-62	$15-18
1950/329	3-Toed Bowl, Scroll	1956-60	$12-15
1950/330	7" Tall Candle Holder (51796)	1955-60, 1977-78	$12-15
1950/331	3 Piece Mayo Set, Scroll	1957-60	$20-32
1950/332	4" Square Bowl, Scroll	1957-60	$10-12
1950/333	Mayo Plate, Scroll	1957-60	$8-10
1950/335	Owl Sugar and Cream	1955-60	$35-40
1950/336	Box and Cover, Grape	1957-62	$18-20
1950/340	Colonial Hat	1955-58	$30-35
1950/342	Puff Box and Cover, Scroll	1956-58	$35-40
1950/???	Little Sleigh Candleholder	? -?	*
1950/346	Little Sleigh (See Photo, p. 144)	? -?	*
1950/347	Sleigh 11" Long (See Photo, p. 145)	1958-59	*
1950/350	Handled Lamp 14"	1962-62	$80-85
1950/356	10" Crimp Vase, Loganberry (51774)	1950-79	$20-25
1950/360D	12" Footed Cake, "Lace Edge Cut"	1956-60	$30-35
1950/360E	12" Footed Banana Stand, "Lace Edge Cut"	1956-60	$35-40
1950/360F	10" Footed Fruit Bowl, "Lace Edge Cut"	1956-60	$35-40
1950/361F	10" Bowl, "Lace Edge Cut"	1956-60	$25-30
1950/362F	8" Bowl, "Lace Edge Cut"	1956-60	$20-25
1950/363F	6" Bowl, "Lace Edge Cut"	1956-60	$15-20
1950/364F	7" Compote, "Lace Edge Cut"	1956-60	$15-17
1950/365B	7" 4-Toed Compote, "Lace Edge Cut"	1956-60	$15-17
1950/366C	6" Candleholder, "Lace Edge Cut"	1956-60	$15-17
1950/367	7 3/4" Basket, "Lace Edge Cut"	1956-60	$35-40
1950/368	12 1/2" Basket, "Lace Edge Cut"	1956-60	$40-50
1950/375	10" Footed Cake Stand, Grape	1958-68	$40-45
1950/376	Wheelbarrow 11 3/4" (See Photo, p. 144)	1958-60	*
1950/377	Pie Wagon and Cover (See Photo, p. 145)	1959-60	$200-225
1950/385	6 3/4" Horseshoe Ash Tray	1956-58	$15-17
1950/396	Salt and Pepper, Scroll	1956-60	$18-20
1950/400	8" Swan	1953-66	$35-40
1950/402	Cigarette Holder	1956-64	$15-18
1950/420	14 Piece Tom and Jerry Set, Black Ladle	1953-55	$200-210
1950/422	Atlantis Cigarette Box, Cover or Desk Box	1950-55	$45-50
1950/425	1-lb. Footed Candy and Cover	1950-64	$22-25
1950/428	Miniature Basket	1950-68	$20-25
1950/433	Syrup Jar and Cover, Grape	1955-64	$18-20
1950/435	6" Partitioned Basket (No Picture)	1959-60	*
1950/450	4 Piece Trivet Ash Tray Set	1950-64	$35-40
1950/451	Trivet Ash Tray, Lyre Of Love	1950-64	$10-12
1950/452	Trivet Ash Tray, Tree Of Life	1950-64	$10-12
1950/453	Trivet Ash Tray, Grape Garden	1950-64	$10-12
1950/454	Trivet Ash Tray, Colonial Eagle	1950-64	$10-12

1950/456	7 1/2" Handled Candy Box and Cover	1957-60	$20-25
1950/457	5" Vase, Spiral	1957-62	$15-20
1950/458	Footed Covered Candy, Fleur-de-lis	1958-60	$28-30
1950/459	Cocktail Pick or Cigarette Holder or Egg Cup	1957-60	$25-30
1950/460	Coach Lamp Candy Box and Cover	1957-59	$40-45
1950/461	Oblong Candy Box, Eagle Finial, Footed	1958-60	$60-65
1950/462	Candy Box and Cover	1957-60	$30-35
1950/463	10" Oval Bowl, " Beaded Rib"	1958-64	$30-35
1950/464	8 1/4" Deep Bowl "Daisy"	1958-62	$30-35
1950/465	9 1/2" Footed Oblong Bowl, "Chain Edge"	1958-62	$28-30
1950/466	5 1/4" Vase	1958-69	$12-15
1950/467	4 1/2" Ivy Jar (No Picture)	1958-68	*
1950/468	4 1/4" Candy Jar & Cover, Grape (51880)	1958-68, 1978-78	$12-15
1950/468C	6 3/4" Bowl, Grape	1959-69	$12-15
1950/471/3	3 Sec Ivy Tower, Grape	1958-68	$35-40
1950/472/4	4 Sec Ivy Tower, Grape	1958-68	$45-50
1950/473	6 oz. Sherbet, Footed, Grape	1951-68	$8-10
1950/473	3 oz. Wine, Grape (11/473)	1943, 1950-68	$10-12
1950/473	9 oz. Tumbler, Grape (11/473)	1943, 1952-64	$8-10
1950/473	12 oz. Tumbler, Grape	1953-71	$8-10
1950/473	10 oz. Goblet, Grape (11/473)	1930s, 1943, 1951-71	$8-18
1950/473	1 Pint Pitcher, Grape	1953-71	$30-35
1950/473	3 Pint Pitcher, Grape (11/473)	1943, 1951-69	$50-55
1950/474C	7" Comporte	1956-62	$15-20
1950/475	Miniature Basket	1959-64	$15-20
1950/478	9 Piece Water Set, Grape (11/473)	1943, 1950-62	$110-120
1950/480	9 1/2" Vase	1956-62	$30-35
1950/486	8 1/2" Masque Vase (11/486C)	1943, 1952-58	$30-35
1950/488	12" Umbrella Vase (11/488)	1930s, 1943	$32-35
1950/488	12" Umbrella Vase (Same as Above) (51775)	1950-59, 1977-78	$32-35
1950/489	8" Basket, Rose Design Interior (See Photo, p. 111)	1968-69	$35-40
1950/489	9 oz. Tumbler, Rose	1950-50	$10-12
1950/493	3 Piece Mayo Set, Grape	1955-69	$22-25
1950/495	Candy Jar and Cover, "Parakeet"	1958-60	$70-75
1950/500	4 Piece Parlor Puppy	1952-52	$140-160
1950/500	15 Piece Punch Set (No Picture)	1955-58	*
1950/505	Cigarette Holder (41624)	1955-68, 1977-78	$15-20
1950/505/1	6 1/2 oz. Cruet and Stopper	1956-60	$25-30
1950/514	9 oz. Tumbler, Windmill	1950-52	$12-15
1950/520	9 1/2" Zodiac Ash Tray	1956-66	$20-22
1950/524	10 1/2" Buffet or Wall Plate, Mum	1950-60	$28-30
1950/525	10 1/2" Plate Homestead	1950-60	$28-30
1950/528	Sugar and Cream "Flower"	1955-58	$15-20
1950/532	7" Ash Tray	1959-69	$15-18
1950/564	8" Pickle	1958-66	$12-15
1950/567	Pineapple Marmalade Jar, Cover and Spoon	1959-65	$40-45
1950/588	Sugar and Cream Set	1955-68	$18-22
1950/595	Sugar and Cream Set	1955-58	$18-22
1950/598	Sugar and Cream Set	1955-58	$18-22
1950/605	6" Wall Pocket Vase, V Shape (See Photo, p. 140)	1959-60	$50-55
1950/607	12" Oval Candle Bowl	1957-62	$25-28
1950/610	7 1/4" Wall Vase, Whisk Broom	1960-60, 1964-68	$50-55
1950/612	4 Piece Toothpick or Cigarette Set	1966-67	$55-60
1950/612	11 1/2" Footed Whisk Broom Vase	1964-66	$25-30
1950/612	8 1/2" 2 Handled Round Comporte	1958-60	$15-18
1950/613	6" Bud Vase, Whisk Broom	1964-68	$15-18
1950/613	9" 2 Handled Comporte	1958-60	$15-18
1950/615	Footed Box and Cover, Hobnail	1964-68	$30-35
1950/615	Footed Box and Cover, Hobnail (Colored Bowl)	1962-62	$40/45
1950/617	Seasoning Shaker Jar and Cover	1963-66	$35-40
1950/617/1	Salt Dip 5 1/4" Tall Flower Bowl (No Picture)	1963-63	$22-25
1950/618	Springerle Box and Cover, Footed	1964-66	$30-35
1950/624	54 oz. Pitcher, Hobnail	1956-59	$45-50
1950/630	8 oz. Goblet, Hobnail	1956-60	$10-12
1950/630	6 oz. Sherbet, Hobnail	1956-60	$10-12
1950/630	12 oz. Ice Tea, Hobnail	1956-60	$12-15
1950/630	10 oz. Tumbler, Hobnail	1956-60	$12-15
1950/630	6 oz. Juice, Hobnail	1956-60	$10-12
1950/631	Footed Sugar and Cream, Hobnail	1957-60	$22-25
1950/635	Candy Box and Cover, Hobnail	1956-60	$20-25
1950/638	8" Plate, Hobnail	1956-60	$8-10
1950/640	4 1/2" Bowl, Hobnail (51680)	1957-59, 1977-78	$8-10
1950/641	8 1/2 Nappy, Hobnail (51696)	1958-59, 1977-78	$15-20
1950/641/2	Salt and Pepper Set, (Glossy Only) (51474)	1978-78	$18-20
1950/642	10" Bowl, Hobnail (51700)	1957-59, 1977-78	$20-22
1950/643	4" Candleholder, Hobnail (51783)	1977-78	$20-22
1950/661	5 1/4" Vase	1956-64	$15-17
1950/662	4 1/2" Vase	1956-60	$12-17
1950/663	4 1/2" Vase Crimp	1956-62	$15-20
1950/666	5 1/2" Handled Box (No Picture)	1958-60	*
1950/678	8 1/2" 2 Handled Pickle	1958-64	$15-18
1950/682	Sugar and Cream Set 3-Toed, Grape	1952-71	$18-20
1950/698	Sugar and Cream, Monticello	1955-58	$18-22
1950/699	6 1/2" Vase, Monticello	1955-60	$18-20
1950/699C	6 1/2" Vase Crimped, Monticello	1956-60	$18-20
1950/700	9 oz. Goblet, "Leaf""	1952-55	$12-15
1950/700	6 oz. Sherbet, "Leaf"	1952-55	$12-15
1950/700	5 1/2 oz. Juice, "Leaf"	1952-55	$12-15
1950/700	12 oz. Footed Ice Tea, "Leaf"	1952-55	$15-20
1950/703D	7" Plate, "Leaf"	1952-55	$8-10
1950/705D	8 1/2" Plate, "Leaf"	1952-55	$10-12
1950/710D	10 1/2" Plate, "Leaf"	1952-55	$15-18
1950/715	Pie Server, Lace Edge (No Picture)	1954-55	*
1950/716	8" Wall Plate, Grape (No Picture)	1954-55	*
1950/717	10" Wall Plate Fruit (No Picture)	1954-55	*
1950/723	3 Piece Mayo, "Leaf"	1952-55	$25-30
1950/727	Footed Candy Box and Cover, Grape	1955-71	$20-22
1950/727C	4" Footed Crimped Bowl, Grape	1958-71	$15-17
1950/730	Sugar and Cream Set, "Leaf"	1952-55	$22-25
1950/735	Hex Candy Box and Cover, Grape	1956-71	$18-20
1950/736	"Butter Pat" Box and Cover (41870)	1964-69, 1977-78	$20-22
1950/737	Cup and Saucer, "Leaf"	1952-55	$15-17
1950/740	Sugar and Cream Set	1955-58	$18-20
1950/741	3 Piece Dresser Set, Hobnail	1956-62	$85-90
1950/742	8" Vase, Hobnail	1953-55	$30-35
1950/743	Box and Cover, Hobnail	1955-62	$28-30
1950/744	Cologne and Stopper, Hobnail	1955-62	$28-30
1950/745C	6" Crimp Bowl, Lace Edge	1953-68	$8-10
1950/745F	6" Bowl, Lace Edge	1953-68	$8-10
1950/746	4 1/4" Crimp Vase, Hobnail (51750)	1956-59, 1972-78	$12-15
1950/749B	7" Comporte, Lace Edge	1954-60	$12-15
1950/749F	7" Comporte, Lace Edge	1954-66	$12-15
1950/749F	7" Comporte, Lace Edge, (Brass Handle)	1962-62	$25-30
1950/750	3 Piece Heart Ash Tray, Candlewick	1950-64	$45-50
1950/752	6 1/2" Fruit, "Leaf"	1952-55	$8-10

Item No.	Description	Years	Price
1950/758	5" Ash Tray	1959-62	$10-12
1950/759	6 1/2" Candy Box and Cover, "Leaf"	1952-55	$15-17
1950/760	Sugar and Cream Set	1955-58	$18-20
1950/765	9" Candy Box and Cover, "Leaf"	1952-55	$20-25
1950/766	11" 3 Candle Float, "Leaf"	1952-55	$20-22
1950/767D	10" Cake Stand, "Leaf"	1952-55	$30-35
1950/767X	11" Footed Fruit, "Leaf"	1952-55	$35-40
1950/772	Sugar and Cream Set, Scroll	1955-60	$20-25
1950/775X	9" Bowl, "Leaf"	1952-55	$22-25
1950/776	Federal Footed Cigarette Holder	1952-55	$40-45
1950/777	Eagle Book End	1955-55	*
1950/778	7" Dolphin Comporte	1954-60	$25-30
1950/779	5" Dolphin Candleholder	1953-60	$15-20
1950/780	3 1/2" Low Candleholder, "Leaf"	1952-55	$15-17
1950/785	6 1/2" Candy Box and Cover, "Leaf Open"	1955-60	$18-20
1950/786	6 1/2" Bowl, "Leaf Open"	1955-60	$8-10
1950/790	Sugar and Cream, Lace Edge	1955-58	$18-20
1950/799	Sugar and Cream, Ivy	1955-58	$18-20
1950/800	Owl Jar and Cover	1955-60	$80-85
1950/801	Cigarette or Tom and Jerry Mug (No Picture)	1953-55	$20-25
1950/805	8 1/2" Celery, Grape	1953-66	$12-15
1950/809	Colonial Belle, 7 1/2" (51844)	1955-58, 1977-78	$35-40
1950/809	Colonial Belle Box	1966-68	$50-55
1950/810	Footed Candy Jar and Cover, Grape	1953-64	$18-20
1950/811	8 1/2" Oval Handled Basket, Grape	1958-60	$45-50
1950/812	8 1/2" Relish Partitioned, Grape	1958-62	$20-22
1950/815	9" Candy Box and Cover, "Leaf Open"	1955-60	$25-30
1950/816	9" Bowl, "Leaf Open"	1955-60	$18-20
1950/817	11 1/4" Fruit Bowl, "Leaf Open"	1956-60	$25-30
1950/818	3 Piece Mayo, "Leaf Open"	1956-60	$25-30
1950/831	Footed Sugar and Cream Set, Grape	1953-69	$20-22
1950/840	11" Candle Float, "Leaf Open"	1956-62	$28-30
1950/842	4 1/2" Handled Nappy, Grape	1953-64	$8-10
1950/851	5" Handled Nappy, Grape (51570)	1953-59, 1978-78	$8-10
1950/858	6" Handled Pickle Tray, Grape	1953-66	$20-22
1950/859	11 1/2" Footed Bowl and Cover, Grape	1956-60	$22-25
1950/860	9 1/2" Footed Bowl and Cover,	1956-60	$30-35
1950/880	3 1/2" Single Candleholder, Grape	1953-70	$10-12
1950/893	Handled Jar and Cover, Wicker Handle, Grape	1953-60	$32-35
1950/895	Heart Wall Pocket (see photo)		*
1950/899	Covered Marmalade, Grape (51580)	1954-68, 1978-78	$15-17
1950/899C	2 Piece Sauce Set, Grape	1957-68	$15-17
1950/900	Covered Sugar & Cream, Grape (51535)	1955-68, 1978-78	$20-22
1950/901	Sugar and Cream, Grape	1955-69	$15-17
1950/906	6 Piece Miniature Lamb Set	1959-60	$100-125
1950/910	7" Whisk Broom Box	1959-60	$20-25
1950/911	Candy Box and Cover (No Picture)	1959-60	*
1950/972	Candy Box and Cover, Toed	1960-62	$35-40
1950/973	Candy Box and Cover, Footed	1959-62	$25-30
1950/974	Footed Candy Box and Cover (51934)	1961-64, 1977-78	$30-35
1950/975	Candy Box and Cover	1961-69	$25-30
1950/976	Footed Candy Box and Cover	1961-69	$25-30
1950/980	5" Pitcher Vase	1960-62	$12-15
1950/981	5" Pitcher Vase	1960-68	$12-15
1950/1602	Cigarette Lighter Cape Cod	1962-66	$40-45
1950/1630	9 Piece Wine Set, Grape (11/473)	1943, 1950-68	$135-140
1950/1723	7 3/4" Basket, Lace Edge	1956-60	$30-35
1950/1725	12 1/2" or 13" Basket, Lace Edge	1956-60	$40-45
1950/1776	6 1/4" Federal Eagle Ash Tray	1952-55	$65-70
1950/2526	Family Sugar and Cream, Rose	1950-60	$30-40
1950/3226	7" Bread and Butter Plate, Scroll	1956-60	$6-8
1950/3227	8" Plate, Scroll	1956-60	$6-8
1950/3228	8 3/4" Plate, Scroll	1956-60	$8-10
1950/3229	9 3/4" Plate, Scroll	1956-60	$10-12
1950/3235	Cup and Saucer, Scroll	1956-60	$15-20
1950/3412	3 Piece Dresser Set, Scroll	1956-58	$105-120
1950/3839	2 Piece Cigarette Set	1954-64	$23-27
1950/4021	4 1/2" Footed Jelly	1958-68	$20-22
1950/4283	Miniature Basket With Salt and Pepper	1950-66	$35-40
1950/4735	6" Plate, Grape	1952-55	$8-10
1950/4736	8" Plate, Grape	1952-55	$10-12
1950/4737	Cup and Saucer, Grape (11/473)	1943, 1951-69	$12-15
1950/4737	Punch Cup, Grape (Same as Above)	1943, 1951-69	$7-8
1950/4738	10" Plate, Grape	1951-55	$18-20
1950/4768	2-Tier Tid Bit Set 12 1/2" Plate and 9" Plate (No Picture)	1950-50	*
1950/5016	Footed Wedding Vase (No Picture)	1957-58	*
1950/5027	2 Piece Hurricane (Cathay Mold)	1954-60	$85-95
1950/7227	3 Piece Dresser, Hobnail	1958-62	$105-120
1950/7243	6" Vase, Hobnail	1957-66	$18-20
1950/7243/1	Bottle and Stopper, Hobnail	1958-62	$30-35
1950/8532	5 Piece Hors D'oeuvre	1951-60	$45-55
11/54	4 1/2" Covered Preserve (1950/156)	1930s	$18-20
11/60	Honey Pot and Cover (1950/60)	1943	$50-55
11/60	Honey Pot and Cover Gold Dec (1950/60)	1943	$50-55
11/100	Boot (1950/101)	1943	$12-15
11/102	Miniature Urn (1950/102)	1943	$12-15
11/103	Miniature Pitcher (1950/104)	1943	$12-15
11/119	Crucifix Candleholder (1950/119)	1943	$80-85
11/145	Chicken On Nest (1950/145)	1930s, 1943	$25-30
11/147	4" Swan (1950/147)	1943	$20-25
11/153	8" Footed Bud Vase	1943	$20-22
11/162	Rabbit On Nest (1950/162)	1943	$25-30
11/473	10" Basket, Grape	1932, 1943	$40-45
11/473	10 oz. Goblet, Grape (1950/473)	1932, 1943	$8-10
11/473	15 Piece Punch Set, Grape (1950/128)	1943	$172-185
11/473	12" Punch Bowl, Grape (1950/128)	1943	$40-50
11/473	5 1/2" Punch Bowl Foot, Grape (1950/128)	1943	$30-35
11/473	Punch Cup, Grape (1950/4737)	1943	$8-10
11/473	9 Piece Wine Set, Grape (1950/1630)	1943	$125-140
11/473	Decanter and Stop, Grape (1950/163)	1932, 1943	$45-50
11/473	2 oz. Wine, Grape (1950/473)	1932, 1943	$10-12
11/473	9 Piece Water Set, Grape (1950/478)	1943	$110-120
11/473	54 oz. Jug, Grape (1950/473)	1932, 1943	$50-55
11/473	10 oz. Tumbler, Grape (1950/473)	1932, 1943	$10-12
11/473	Cup and Saucer, Grape (1950/4737)	1932, 1943	$12-15
11/473	8" Blown Vase, Grape (No Picture)	1932	*
11/473C	6" Footed Compote, Grape	1932, 1943	$12-15
11/486C	9" Vase Crimped (1950/486)	1943	$30-35
11/488	12" Blown Vase (1950/488)	1932, 1943	$32-35
11/592	Tom and Jerry Bowl, Gold Decorated.	1935, 1943	$60-65
11/592	Tom and Jerry Mug, Gold Decorated	1935, 1943	$10-12
11/699	Tall Footed Candy Jar, Washington	1943	$40-45
11/739	Card or Cigarette Holder With Dog	1930s	$30-35
11/742	Footed Ivy Ball, Hobnail	1930s, 1943	$25-30
11/742	Puff Box and Cover, Hobnail	1932	$28-30
11/742	Cologne and Stopper, Hobnail	1932	$28-30
11/742	6 Piece Dresser Set, Hobnail	1932	$85-90
11/742C	7" Compote, Hobnail, (51720)	1943, 1977-78	$18-20
11/742N	Footed Ivy Bowl, Hobnail (1950/188)	1943	$25-27
11/743B	5 1/4" Vase, Lace Edge	1930s	$12-15
11/743K	5" Vase, Lace Edge	1930s	$12-15
11/743N	5 1/2" Vase, Lace Edge	1930s	$12-15
11/743X	4 1/2" Vase, Lace Edge	1930s	$12-15
11/775	10" Blown Vase	1930s, 1943	$20-25
11/4021	4 1/2" Footed Jelly	1930s	$12-15
11/4731	8" Vase, Grape	1930s	*

11/4731C	9" Vase, Grape (1950/287)	1943	$25-30
11/4732B	6" Vase, Grape	1930s, 1943	$12-15
11/4732N	6" Vase, Grape	1930s	$20-22
11/4732K	6" Vase, Grape	1943	$20-22
11/4736C	8 3/4" Crimped Plate, Grape	1932	$20-25
11/4736C	9 1/2" Dish, Grape	1930s, 1943	$20-25
11/4738C	10 1/2" Crimped Fruit Bowl, Grape	1943	$45-50
11/4738C	10 1/2" Crimped Fruit Bowl and Stand, Grape	1943	$70-75
11/4738D	12" Plate, Grape	1943	$25-30
11/4738D	12" Cake Plate On Stand 2 Piece, Grape	1943	$45-50
11/4738N	8" Bulb Bowl, Grape	1943	$35-40
11/4738N	8" Bulb Bowl On Stand, Grape	1943	$70-75
11/7003/4	4 1/2" Fruit Nappy, Grape	1932	$10-12
11/7003/4	6" Plate, Grape	1932	$10-12
11/7005/4	8" Salad Plate, Grape	1932	$10-12
11/7005/4	6 1/2" Nappy, Grape	1932	$10-12
11/7007/4	11" Service Plate, Grape, (Same as 11/7003/4)	1932	$15-20
11/7007/4	9" Fruit Bowl, Grape	1932	$15-20
11/7423C	7 1/2" Blown Vase, Hobnail	1930s	$30-35
11/7445D	7 1/2" Plate, Lace Edge	1930s	$8-10
11/7455B	6 1/2" Bell Bowl, Lace Edge	1932	$8-10
11/7455D	7 1/2" Plate, Lace Edge	1932	$8-10
11/7455F	7" Shallow Bowl, Lace Edge (1950/207F)	1932	$10-15
11/7455G	6" Basket Bowl, Lace Edge	1932	$10-15
11/7850	Covered Cigarette Box	1930s	$30-35
1950/1186	4 1/2" Blown Vase		*
1591	Story Book Mug (51320)	1978-78	$40-45
51480	Salt and Pepper, Hobnail (Glossy Only) (51480)	1977-78	$20-25
51599	9" Pickle "Loves Request" (51599)	1978-78	$20-30
91	Punch Ladle, Crystal		$45-50
128	Punch Ladle, Christmas Green	1950	$70-75
	Punch Ladle, Black	1953	$70-75
	5 1/4" Mayo Ladle, Milk Glass	1950	$10-12
	5 1/2" Mayo Ladle, Black	1953-56	$15-17

Index

This index contains the names of decorations, patterns, categories, and specific items that are easily identified by the shape and design of the milk glass piece.

American Jars, 15, 44, 146
Antiqued Milk Glass, 33
Animals, 49, 57, 65, 117, 118, 119, 120
Atterbury Dove Box and Cover, 18, 120
Atterbury Lion Box and Cover, 18, 119
Atterbury Molds, 18, 19
Baskets, 121
Belknap Collection, 17
Black Glass, 35, 36, 47, 48, 49
Boot, 146
Boudoir Items, 6, 36, 45, 68, 97, 100, 115, 130, 131, 134, 146
Bundling Lamp, 128, 129
Bunny-on Nest, 118, 119
Candleholder, 128, 129
Candlewick, 20, 22, 47, 70, 71, 72, 76, 77, 78
Cape Cod, 79, 80
Cased Banjo and Fiddle, 63
Chroma #123, 73
Cigarette Items, 130, 131, 132
Coach Lamp, 27, 28, 29, 30, 126
Colonial Belle, 145, 147
Colonial Hat, 144, 146
Colonial Rose, 20
Comportes and Condiments, 133, 134
Cornucopia, 144, 146
Cream and Sugar Sets Decorated, 23, 24
Cream and Sugar Sets, 23, 24, 136, 137, 138
Crucifix Candleholder, 129
Diamond Block #330, 73
Doeskin, 15
Dolphin, 129, 134
Duck-on-Nest, 117, 119
Eagle Bookend, 118, 120
End O'Day, 50, 57
Gold Encrusted Band, 20
Gold Flecked, 31, 32
Gold Scroll and Rose, 21
Grape, 81, 82, 83, 84, 85, 86, 87, 88, 89, 90, 91, 92, 93, 94, 95, 96
Grape, Hand Decorated, 26
Heart Shaped Candy Box and Cover, 126
Heisey Animals, 65
Hen-on-Nest, 119
Hobby Horse, 21, 119
Hobnail, 61, 97, 98, 99, 100, 101
Honey Jar, 22
Intaglio, 16
Knife Rest, 147
Lace Edge, 102, 103, 104, 105, 106
Lace Edge Cut, 103, 107
Lamb Set, 147
Lamps, 129, 130
Leaf, 108, 109, 110
Leaf Open, 108, 110
Loganberry Vase, 139, 142, 143
Love Bird Vase, 141, 143
Metal
    Colonial Black Iron, 42
    Golden Brass, 37, 38, 39
    Wrought Iron, 40, 41
Metropolitan Museum of Art, 69
Monticello #698, 141
Murrhina, 34
Opaque Glass
    Forget-Me-Not-Blue, 43, 44, 46
    Midwest Custard, 43, 44, 45, 46

    Turquoise, 43, 44, 45, 46
Owl Jar and Cover, 19, 120
Owl Sugar and Cream, 136, 138
Parakeet Candy Jar and Cover, 127
Parlor Puppy, 118, 120
Peach Blow, 62
Pear Candy Jar and Cover, 126
Pennsylvania Dutch—Peasant Art, 21, 22
Pillsbury Cook Book, 71
Pie Wagon, 145
Pineapple Candy Jar and Cover, 125
Pineapple Marmalade Jar and Cover, 134
Private Mold Customers, 9, 67
    Butler Brothers, 47
    Irving W. Rice, 67, 68
    Metropolitan Museum of Art, 69
    F.W. Woolworth, Company, 69
    Hotel and Restaurant Trade, 69
    Smithsonian Institute, 69
Polychrome, 20
Provincial 58, 59
Provincial, Parisian, 60
Rabbit Box and Cover, 118, 119
Rabbit, Covered, 119
Reeded #701, 36
Rooster Box and Cover, 118, 119
Rooster Egg Cup, 120
Rose, 75, 111, 112
Salt and Pepper Sets, 136, 137, 138
Scroll, 113, 114, 115
Ski Tumbler, 74
Slag Glass
    Blue, 57
    Caramel, 50, 51, 53, 55, 57, 72
    Jade, 50, 51, 52, 53, 54
    Purple, 50, 51, 54, 55
    Ruby, 50, 51, 52, 53, 54, 55, 56
Sleigh, 144, 145
Smithsonian Institution, 69
Story Book Mug, 147
Sugar and Cream Sets Decorated. See Cream and Sugar Sets Decorated
Sugar and Cream Sets. See Cream and Sugar Sets
Swan, 120
Swan Mint Whimsy, 117, 119
Swan-on-Nest, 118, 119
Swung Vases, 66
Table Lamp, 75
Toast and Cover, 84
Tom and Jerry Set, 93, 135
Toothpick #505, 150
Tradition #165, 72
Turkey-on-Nest, 117, 119
Vase, 139, 140, 141, 142, 143
Vigna Vetro, 34
Vinelf, 128, 129, 133
Violets, Hand Decorated, 25
Wall Pocket, 140, 141, 143
Washington #669, 73, 127
Watch Candy Box and Cover, 126
Wassail Set, 93
Wheelbarrow, 144
White Ice, 64
Windmill, 115, 116